Operating Continuously

Best Practices for Accelerating Software Delivery

Edith Harbaugh, Cody De Arkland, and Brian Rinaldi

Beijing · Boston · Farnham · Sebastopol · Tokyo

Operating Continuously

by Edith Harbaugh, Cody De Arkland, and Brian Rinaldi

Copyright © 2023 O'Reilly Media. All rights reserved.

Published by O'Reilly Media, Inc., 1005 Gravenstein Highway North, Sebastopol, CA 95472.

O'Reilly books may be purchased for educational, business, or sales promotional use. Online editions are also available for most titles (*http://oreilly.com*). For more information, contact our corporate/institutional sales department: 800-998-9938 or *corporate@oreilly.com*.

Acquisitions Editor: Melissa Duffield	**Indexer:** nSight, Inc.
Development Editor: Gary O'Brien	**Interior Designer:** Monica Kamsvaag
Production Editor: Beth Kelly	**Cover Designer:** Susan Thompson
Copyeditor: Arthur Johnson	**Illustrator:** Kate Dullea
Proofreader: Shannon Turlington	

April 2023:   First Edition

Revision History for the First Edition

2023-04-10:   First Release

See *http://oreilly.com/catalog/errata.csp?isbn=9781098117290* for release details.

978-1-098-11729-0

[LSI]

Contents

Preface

—Edith Harbaugh

The software delivery space is changing rapidly. The goal remains the same—to produce quality software that helps customers and businesses—but the way to achieve that goal continues to evolve.

This book's predecessor, *Effective Feature Management* (*https://oreil.ly/grD3A*) (O'Reilly), was released in February 2019. Since then, many of the technologies involved in delivery have evolved. Maturation in tooling has led to a complete shift in how teams engage and operate in this space. This shift and other global developments, such as the shift to remote work and the increase of cloud adoption, have changed the way software teams work in 2023.

The traditional divisions and handoffs in software delivery among product management, design, development, operations, and analysis have become democratized and more collaborative. Historically, these teams have operated in siloed verticals, focusing on tasks impacting their specific workstreams in a step-by-step, waterfall fashion. The rise of Agile, DevOps, and continuous delivery broke down barriers, and now there's a next wave of *operating continuously* in which leading organizations are forming integrated teams for even closer collaboration to produce high-quality, less risky software. Software development is truly a team effort. This book will explore this concept and give you a closer view into how organizations are adopting an operating continuously mindset and the pitfalls they may encounter along the way.

Who Will Benefit from Reading This Book?

This book is targeted primarily at technical leaders across development, operations, and product management roles, as well as CTOs and architecture leaders who are dealing with common struggles related to the typical Agile development model and are looking for guidance in moving beyond it. They have firsthand experience with the pains of software development occurring in iterations across disparate teams and in parallel to other groups. Our book aims to help them devise strategies to ease or eliminate these pains.

Technical practitioners within the same groups referenced above can also benefit from the insights in this book if they are looking to understand more about roles and processes that exist beyond their team. For example, a product manager might not have visibility into the trials and tribulations within the typical operations role. Reviewing *Chapter 3, "Operate"*, can provide greater insight into the key components of this role and into how they can work better together.

Organizations are often very different from one another. As authors, we've done our best to align the content within this book to the majority of organizations, but as always, the complexities of individual organizations, verticals, and even teams can often result in varying levels of ease and friction around concepts within this book.

Navigating and Using This Book

This book mainly concerns the operations side of software delivery. We, the authoring team, have structured it into four chapters focusing successively on the *deploy*, *release*, *operate*, and *measure and experiment* stages:

- In *Chapter 1, "Deploy"*, we'll explain the characteristics of healthy deployment practices, which should minimize the time to go from local development to production, provide a platform from which you can easily visualize and manage what change is landing in production, and allow you to roll rapidly backward or forward as necessary. We'll introduce the argument that smaller and more frequent deployments are better than larger, less frequent ones—especially when you can leverage development practices like feature flagging to mitigate risk. We'll also look at deployment orchestration and discuss the relative merits of different deployment strategies.

- In *Chapter 2, "Release"*, we'll explain how to leverage approaches like feature management to make release a separate step from deployment. We'll cover use cases, including kill switches, progressive rollouts, progressive delegation, testing in production, and personalization. And we'll discuss the personas, tools, and collaboration necessary to utilize these strategies.

- In *Chapter 3, "Operate"*, we'll introduce the new activities that we see integrated software teams leveraging to understand and act on a system in operation. We'll touch on incident management practices that we see being adopted to support continuous operation. Finally, we'll explore the importance of personnel and how you organize teams.

- In continuous operation, measurement and experimentation are key functions of numerous roles working in concert. In *Chapter 4, "Measure and Experiment"*, we'll cover A/B/n testing and product analytics, paying special attention to governance and clean data. We'll also introduce the concept of release impact, which is distinct from optimization-focused experimentation.

While we have written this book as an end-to-end flow, it can also be used as a reference guide, with each section providing clarity, offering recommendations, and outlining pitfalls to avoid within each domain.

Conventions Used in This Book

The following typographical conventions are used in this book:

Italic
> Indicates new terms, URLs, filenames, and file extensions.

`Constant width`
> Used for program listings, as well as within paragraphs to refer to program elements such as variable or function names, databases, data types, environment variables, statements, and keywords.

O'Reilly Online Learning

 For more than 40 years, *O'Reilly Media* has provided technology and business training, knowledge, and insight to help companies succeed.

Our unique network of experts and innovators share their knowledge and expertise through books, articles, and our online learning platform. O'Reilly's online learning platform gives you on-demand access to live training courses, in-depth learning paths, interactive coding environments, and a vast collection of text and video from O'Reilly and 200+ other publishers. For more information, visit *https://oreilly.com*.

How to Contact Us

Please address comments and questions concerning this book to the publisher:

O'Reilly Media, Inc.

1005 Gravenstein Highway North

Sebastopol, CA 95472

800-998-9938 (in the United States or Canada)

707-829-0515 (international or local)

707-829-0104 (fax)

We have a web page for this book, where we list errata, examples, and any additional information. You can access this page at *https://oreil.ly/operating-continuously*.

Email *bookquestions@oreilly.com* to comment or ask technical questions about this book.

Visit *https://oreilly.com* for news and information about our books and courses.

Find us on LinkedIn: *https://linkedin.com/company/oreilly-media*

Follow us on Twitter: *https://twitter.com/oreillymedia*

Watch us on YouTube: *https://youtube.com/oreillymedia*

Acknowledgments

I'd like to thank my coauthors Cody De Arkland and Brian Rinaldi for their help in writing this book. In addition, special thanks are due to Peter McCarron, Zach Davis, and Robert Neal for their help reviewing and editing specific sections throughout, Seth Mazow for his research and additions, and the other employees at LaunchDarkly who have provided me with context along the way.

I'd also like to thank LaunchDarkly cofounder and CTO John Kodumal for his friendship throughout our journey together. He dedicated his PhD thesis to me, and I am repaying him.

Finally, I'd like to thank LaunchDarkly customers for giving us the opportunity to partner with them on their operational transformations. Their experiences since 2014 have given us the knowledge to write this book.

Introduction

—Edith Harbaugh

Operating continuously is the nirvana of software development—a software delivery lifecycle in which planning, coding, building, testing, releasing, deploying, operating, and monitoring processes unite to produce value for end users and less stress and risk for those building the software. We are in a transition phase from traditional project-oriented waterfall processes to product-oriented continuous processes. This transition is exciting but, like any change, also scary. I hope this book explains this natural evolution and gives you examples of cultures, processes, and tooling that can help you successfully embrace operating continuously.

I started my career in the '90s, working first as a software analyst/designer and then as an engineering program manager, when software was made in rigid waterfall processes. The product manager wrote a product requirement doc (PRD), which I, the analyst/designer in engineering, then translated into use cases and functional requirements (known as *functional requirement specifications*). Designers would make mock-ups, which engineers would subsequently implement. There were then several rounds of quality assurance (QA) to check for user acceptance (did the product manager think it functioned?), defects, and platform compatibility, since customers were installing the software on their own systems. Part of my role as program manager was to generate and maintain the *supported platform matrix*, which identified which combinations (and what versions) of operating systems, databases, and application servers were supported.

Shipping in the 1990s and early 2000s was an exercise in evaluating where in the triangle of scope, quality, and time the software was. If there were sufficient features and low enough defects (coupled with pressure from sales and marketing), a release would be deemed "ready." Following that was a release-to-manufacturing stage in which the bits would be put up on a website for customers to download and install. Since customers adopted a new version probably only once a year or so unless they urgently needed a new feature or bug fix, there was much angst about what level of defects was acceptable, not to mention which features to build to begin with. All of this led to more and more documentation about requirements, and longer and longer release processes, due to software teams trying to pack in new features and bug fixes. As a result, software releases sometimes shipped not just months but *years* late, completely missing the mark for customers. *Duke Nukem Forever* (*https://oreil.ly/ih29Q*) is legendary for being 14 years in development.

The tandem rise of Agile and the cloud radically changed software development. If customers didn't have to download and install a release, but rather the software was hosted, you could release frequently—not just once a year or once a quarter, but literally every minute. In 2001 the authors of the Agile Manifesto preached these four virtues:[1]

- Individuals and interactions over processes and tools
- Working software over comprehensive documentation
- Customer collaboration over contract negotiation
- Responding to change over following a plan

The combination of being able to release more quickly due to cloud hosting and a methodology that explicitly rewarded "responding to change" naturally resulted in software organizations rethinking how they viewed software development. This rethinking led to DevOps and to new software lifecycle methodologies such as the DevOps infinity loop, which represents the stages that take place during software development (see *Figure I-1*).

The software industry has focused an enormous amount of effort on the steps that precede release in the DevOps infinity loop. The Agile movement, the adoption of continuous integration/continuous delivery (CI/CD), and the introduction of DevOps have led to a set of modern practices that take software from concept to "ready to deploy." While these practices have given us new ways to quickly develop and ship software, they've also created challenges in the ways these processes move between teams, and in the model itself. Entire solutions have been created around each stage in the infinity loop, but what if the problem

---

1 Kent Beck et al. 2001. "Manifesto for Agile Software Development" (*https://oreil.ly/W2CxE*).

isn't the individual steps? What if the real problem is that the step-by-step model that the DevOps infinity loop represents has become outdated?

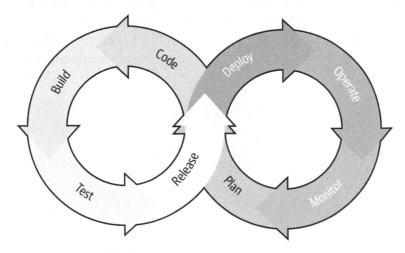

Figure I-1. The DevOps infinity loop

The next stage of evolution in software delivery is happening now. Cutting-edge software teams are developing and introducing new tools, technologies, and processes that extend continuous delivery beyond the deployment stage into software that's live and running in production. No longer sequential handoffs, these interactions are instead often running as continuous processes within their own stages. I refer to this model as *continuous operation*.

The practice of DevOps largely grew from the learnings of software development teams, which were applied to broader operations throughout organizations. Similar to how infrastructure teams evolved to adopt developer practices, continuous operation improves the efficiency of the teams involved in operating software platforms. This book documents these shifts and provides guidance for how teams can adopt the approach of continuous operations. We'll explore the specific stages and areas of the software delivery model and provide guidance on:

- The discrete steps in continuous operation and how they fit together
- The tools, processes, and people needed to make each step continuous
- The business value continuous operation provides

As we detail these emerging practices, it will become clear how important it is to revisit the way teams are building and shipping software and to rethink existing models, such as the DevOps infinity loop and the traditional software development lifecycle (SDLC) model. The end result is a refreshed framework that takes a continuous approach to the key components of software delivery, focusing on deploy, release, operate, and measure and experiment (see *Figure I-2*).

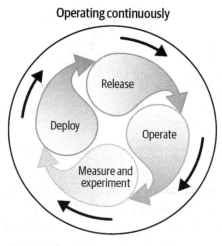

Figure I-2. Operating continuously

Continuous operation has three distinct differences from earlier models:

It's not just about dev and ops
> Additional personas, including product managers, designers, security managers, and more, have a role in monitoring and operating software in production.

The steps need a refresh
> When viewed narrowly as a DevOps task, the idea of release as a packaging step that occurs before deployment is dated, as is the idea of monitoring.

The steps happen in parallel
> Unlike the left side of the DevOps infinity loop, where, for example, planning precedes development, the steps of continuous operation all happen in parallel while the system is in operation.

It's Never Been Just About Dev and Ops

One of the stated goals of the DevOps movement is to reduce siloing and handoffs. By integrating the practices of developers and operations teams, we can create teams with shared objectives and responsibilities. We can collaborate continuously and eliminate the step-by-step processes and dependencies that create the "baton handoff" motion between teams.

Note

For the purposes of this book, we'll use the generic term *integrated software delivery team*, or simply *software delivery team*, to refer to an organizational structure that integrates all the functions within the software development lifecycle into a collaborative unit.

Developers do not build software in isolation. When I worked as a product manager at TripIt in the 2010s, my team comprised myself, a designer, and engineers. This model of operation is commonly referred to as a *squad* model, where a cross-functional team comes together to develop as an integrated team. Increasingly in the 2020s, security and operations are baked into every step of the process instead of being bolted on at the end.

One of the key observations I've made in my career in engineering, product, and marketing and as a founder of LaunchDarkly is that high-performing software teams invite significantly more members into the software delivery team. These expanded teams can often include broader stakeholders across development, operations, product management, security, and other areas, engaging them in observing, controlling, monitoring, and measuring what happens in production software. In other words, continuous operation is a shared responsibility for the entire software delivery team, not just developers and operations. For example, developers can use runtime error monitoring software to detect bugs. Operations engineers use observability tools to measure performance and mitigate incidents. But in addition to that, product managers can use feature management tools to control feature releases and run experiments. Designers can use session replay software to observe user interactions and improve end-user experiences. Security engineers can use threat monitoring tools to continuously monitor security risk. The continuous operation of a software product across an integrated software delivery team creates incredibly efficient feedback loops and rapid responses to change failure, incidents, and other forms of risk.

When you consider the ways these teams interact with one another in an integrated software delivery team and then try to fit that interaction into the sequential model represented by the infinity loop, the challenges in that legacy model immediately become visible.

The Steps Need a Refresh

The idea of release before deploy, as depicted in the DevOps infinity loop image in *Figure I-1*, has been updated. In the previous model, development teams would build their software independently, testing locally and in their own environments. Upon that code becoming "development complete," the code would be handed off to the teams responsible for building and packaging the code. This metaphorical baton-pass represented the handoff to "code release" before actual deployment out to destination infrastructure. Postdeployment, the baton would then be passed to QA teams to validate the success of the build.

Release processes in this model involved release managers who would decide what was included in a release and eventually distributed out to users. While this model is still relevant (e.g., for firmware, operating systems, and open source libraries), software as a service (SaaS) models demand and thrive in a more continuous process. This enables a more concurrent model of deployment and release, which can be improved even further by leveraging feature management platforms to separate the deployment process from the release process. The separation allows the release process to become a more continuous operation of its own, independent of continuous integration/deployment.

Shifting to a continuous operation also forces us to shift our thinking around many of the stages involved in the SDLC. A great example is the monitoring step (which I cover in greater detail later in this book). In traditional organizations, the task of monitoring is typically a function of operations teams ensuring the availability of a system, implying a specific function performed by a specific team.

Continuous operation, however, involves more stakeholders, and it's necessary to expand our notion of monitoring appropriately to reflect the concerns of those stakeholders. While monitoring accurately reflects the needs of operations engineers concerned with availability, it doesn't encompass product managers monitoring user behaviors and running A/B tests and experiments, or growth teams monitoring the impact of changes on their key performance indicators (KPIs). In short, it's too limited a notion to capture everything that broader integrated software delivery teams watch postdeployment and postrelease. I believe *measuring and experimenting* is a better name for this stage; it encapsulates the need to quantitatively observe and react to both system and user behaviors occurring in a production system. In continuous operation, everyone involved in the software release measures relevant aspects of their domain, and does so continuously.

The Steps Happen in Parallel

One of the differences between the pre- and postdeployment steps in the SDLC is that in postdeployment, all steps happen in parallel. The DevOps infinity loop implies that the loop is continuous (meaning a cycle in which the process continues and repeats as teams iterate on what they've built). However, it's still restrictive in that it implies that the handoffs happen sequentially. In truth, many of these steps have evolved to have their own continuous loops within the DevOps loop—resulting in this model of continuous operation. For a given product change, predeployment steps have a defined sequence. In other words, planning occurs before implementation.

In contrast, the stages we're introducing as essential in continuous operation all happen concurrently. There are no sequential steps postdeployment because modern software services are always running. When teams deploy, they are upgrading the airplane while it's in flight. They're constantly measuring everything about the system, constantly deploying changes to it, and constantly reacting to changing inputs and traffic. These factors necessitate that they be able to measure, react, and control the system quickly—ideally in real time, so that they can adapt to changing conditions.

When the traditional SDLC diagram is updated with our proposed changes, the result looks something like *Figure I-3*.

What do these changes look like in practice? What tools and processes facilitate continuous operation? In this book, we'll cover each stage of continuous operation and share observations on emerging best practices and tools.

Software development has changed dramatically in the 25 years since my first programming job in Visual Basic. Software is more omnipresent in how businesses operate. As software has become how the world runs, the roles involved in software development, the timing of tasks, and the tools that are utilized have all evolved. With changes in people, processes, and ways of working together, a new framework is needed to visualize the modern ways teams ship and deliver software. This book aims to spell out a refreshed framework for visualizing this lifecycle.

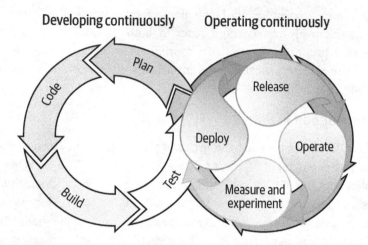

Figure I-3. The updated software delivery model

Deploy

The *deploy* stage (see *Figure 1-1*) represents taking code that has been developed and packaged and shipping it to a destination for user consumption. It's the result of local development becoming shippable code. Development teams value code that's been shipped to the dev environment—but ultimately the organizational value is still low. As code gets closer and closer to production environments—where end users can consume and interact with it—the value (and ultimately the risk) increases.

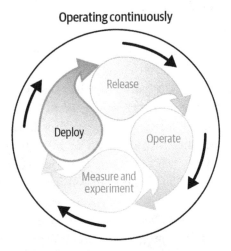

Figure 1-1. The deploy stage

One of the most outdated aspects of the DevOps infinity loop is that release precedes deploy. This sequencing can be traced back to the idea that once a build of software code was "development complete" (i.e., all development on specific changes was done), the code would be released into the build processes. This definition not only no longer holds true but also is too restrictive for the speed and scale at which teams need to build and ship their software. It's also worth noting that in this context, we're using *release* to refer to the activity of releasing software and not to the actual version of a software release.

In modern software development, the deployment process covers the workflow of moving compiled code onto a destination infrastructure or software platform. While this is roughly reflected in the infinity loop chart, the methods of facilitating that deployment process have matured and changed.

This chapter will sharpen the deployment story and provide more clarity on the ways in which teams are now deploying software. This includes:

- What deployment previously meant and what it means now
- Techniques and approaches to improve deployment velocity
- The roles involved in deploying code in multiple scenarios

Redefining Release and Deploy

In organizations that are embracing the practice of continuous operations, the release of software functionality to end users ultimately ends up taking place after the software deployment has occurred—when software teams want to enable feature or functionality consumption by those groups. In this example, it becomes necessary for the actual software code to be deployed onto the destination environment in order for that feature or functionality to be available for release. Deployment, whether to production or to any other environment, no longer requires or even implies a release. Deployed code is dropped into an environment, where it is evaluated and prepared for having its features released for consumption by end users.

These feature changes can be released to small groups of employees, to specific users as part of a beta program, or to all users in a general availability (GA) release. The responsibility for deciding which feature (or code) gets released to a configured group, and when, can be shared among people with different job titles across the software delivery team. We will expand on this group of decision makers in later chapters, but ultimately this becomes the foundation of continuous release—the idea that teams can constantly be releasing new features to users or groups, independent of or unconstrained by the existing deployment process.

WHAT DEPLOY AND RELEASE USED TO MEAN

It's worth noting that software releases used to be giant packages of many features (small and large), small bug fixes, and everything in between. The dev half of the DevOps infinity loop showed how an organization created new software and, when the software was deemed complete, it was packaged together as a release. These collections of changes were commonly created at regularly set intervals, such as annually or quarterly. For code to be accepted into a seasonal or annual release, it had to be tested in conjunction with both the existing software and the new code in that particular release. If code was not complete or didn't pass the integration tests, it didn't make it into that release and had to wait for the next release cycle.

Once the bundle of changes that made it into a new release was packaged up, it would then be deployed or distributed out to the necessary endpoints. *Deploy* in this case meant "put in the field." This is why the deploy stage comes after the release stage in the traditional DevOps infinity loop chart—because you couldn't deploy software that hadn't been released yet.

Deployment and release have been historically tied together, mostly because of infrastructure considerations. Code was included in a software release, which was distributed and fully tested in lower environments such as testing or staging, which typically leveraged dedicated infrastructure. Once success was validated in these lower environments, the software release was ready to be deployed to broader user groups by moving it onto the production environment/infrastructure. At this point, the existing, live application would have to be placed into some form of maintenance mode (taken offline), typically during off-hours, to push the new release code out. Once everything was validated as working in production, the app was made available again, and the release was completed.

WHAT DEPLOY AND RELEASE MEAN NOW

As organizations have shifted how they build and ship software, the meaning of release has changed. Continuous integration (CI) and continuous delivery (CD) give organizations the ability to continuously deploy code changes across multiple environments, without dedicated release managers and build teams handcrafting releases. Nightly builds are commonplace, with many organizations even moving past "nightly" into continuous patterns in which changes are built and deployed at the time of commit, especially in SaaS environments. With new software builds compiled and deployed at this rate of change, the idea of deploy no longer needs to be tied directly to the traditional release concept. With software now being continuously integrated (built/tested/packaged) and continuously deployed (shipped to one or many destination infrastructures or platforms) in a much-simplified process, the implied meaning of what a release is also changes.

Introducing the practice and tooling of feature management gives teams fine-grained control over releasing their code (features) that has already been deployed into an environment. Leveraging feature flags allows teams to gate their newly developed code and control whether that change is available to end users. The old definition of a software release shifts to become more aligned with the term *software build*, and release shifts to the actions software teams take to make functionality available to end users and systems (i.e., the feature flag/toggle experience). Releases are no longer a software artifact or a set of binary files shipped to a destination; furthermore, they can be controlled through targeting rules, as well as the practice of canary deployments (also sometimes called canary rollouts or canary releases), to allow releases to be made available progressively, on a sliding scale. The end result is that teams have far greater control over feature releases and their overall impact—an outcome that truly aligns with the overall focus of DevOps principles.

Now that we've outlined the new deploy and release framework, let's explore the evolved approach to the deployment strategies themselves, such as how organizations are realizing the benefits of releasing small batches frequently.

SMALL AND FREQUENT > LARGE AND INFREQUENT

As teams look to transform how software is shipped, the optimal deployment pace within an environment focuses on a high frequency of small software deployments (software deployments shipped to the infrastructure the software runs on). Shipping at high velocity has numerous benefits:

Small batch sizes
> Since each deployment is small, the raw speed of the deployment itself can be minimized.

Easy problem diagnosis
> If something goes wrong, looking at the recent deployments and their associated code changes is a simpler task than trying to decompose larger builds with many code changes. Since deployments are small, deciphering what each deployment does and how it might have caused the problem is straightforward (especially when tied to feature flag usage, which will be covered more in later chapters).

Speed to market

Deploying frequently means you are in a constant state of forward motion with your product. You're making frequent incremental improvements or corrections, resulting in your customers receiving a better product.

Merge conflict minimization

Large batches make merge conflicts inevitable and hard to untangle. Small and frequent code commits minimize merge conflicts since there is less time for code to become stale.

High team morale

In organizations that have invested culturally in the "small and frequent" approach, the deployment process is often optimized, allowing developers to do what they love: building and shipping code. Infrequent deployments cause developers to spend more time dealing with merge conflicts, giving them less time to work on the next deployment.

Infrequent deployments tend to be larger and more complex, so when an issue arises, figuring out which change(s) caused a problem can be challenging, leading to a more time-intensive incident process (often in the middle of an active incident). The longer an incident drags on, the more likely that tempers flare, tertiary stakeholders start demanding information, and the impact grows throughout other connected systems and even the organization as a whole.

Culturally, an infrequent deployment posture frustrates developers, ultimately reducing developer satisfaction, and can even cause employee attrition in many cases. Developers want to see progress in their work and not be blocked by endless code reviews on large code changes, merge conflict resolution, and challenging deployment processes. Organizations that deploy quickly will successfully attract and retain engineering talent. It's a virtuous cycle. Considering the high cost of recruiting and paying developers, doing anything that hinders their output should be avoided at all costs.

Frequent deployments don't just achieve success in an isolated section of the DevOps infinity loop. They directly influence every subsequent section of the DevOps cycle. If deployments to production are frequent, small, and reversible (via feature flags), the rest of your software development process will be set up for success. The opposite is true as well. If the deployment process is slow and batch sizes are high, releases will be infrequent, and incidents will have more severity.

Note

The key takeaway: small, frequent releases make problem diagnosis easier, increase speed to market, minimize merge conflicts, and improve the morale of your development team.

DEPLOY CAN BE DECOUPLED FROM RELEASE

One of the fundamental ways to speed up the deployment process is to separate it from the release process. In the old model, deploy and release were glued together. Whatever was in "the winter release" was accessible to all users at the same time.

If deploying code to production means that all users immediately see the new functionality, the stakes for every deployment activity are extremely high. These higher stakes in many cases translate to more testing, code reviews, and process burden, which will inevitably lead to a slower deployment frequency.

To achieve the benefits of continuous delivery, release has to be separated from deploy. If code can be deployed to production, and the visibility of that feature is controlled, then the stakes are lower and the requisite testing procedures can be less intensive, especially when combined with release targeting. Release targeting allows teams to explicitly target a portion of their code at a specific grouping of individuals or systems. The product team can run beta programs and canary rollouts during the release process, gradually releasing features to select groups. A streaming service can target specific device types with a new set of code.

From a development methodology perspective, feature flags are one of the best avenues to decouple the activity of deployment from release. A change can be deployed to production but have its feature flag set to "off" for some or all users, rendering the change inactive. In this example, code has been deployed to the production environment, and the releasing of that feature or capability to the user community is an independent process occurring after the deployment.

When the product team finds issues within the deployment, it also has the ability to immediately (and independently) disable the problem code by way of a kill switch—a rollback strategy that is available when you're developing with feature flags. If deploy and release are tied together, a rollback of problematic code risks giving users whiplash when new features suddenly disappear across the entire user community. Such a poor user experience can cause disruption and frustration and ultimately lead to customer churn.

MERGE CONFLICTS AND THEIR IMPACT ON DEPLOYMENTS

In the practice of software development, specifically when you are working in source control, code branches are frequently created for developers to build new software capabilities. The longer these branches exist apart from the main branch, the higher the risk that they become so diverged that conflicts in the codebase emerge as changes are committed and merged into the main trunk from other branches. These merge conflicts are costly to resolve from both a time and a developer productivity perspective. This time to resolve inhibits the ability of teams to ship newly built code into their environments. Developers are forced to pause development while they resolve the conflicts, distracting them from the core goal of shipping code.

At a high enough frequency, time and productivity loss can compound, causing far-reaching impacts on job satisfaction, developer retention, and operational efficiency. Conversely, an organization that is committing code often, with frequent code merges into the main trunk, experiences a greatly reduced risk of these merge conflicts due to the short-lived nature of the branches. With fewer merge conflicts to resolve, another barrier is removed from the opportunity to embrace a more continuous model, especially within the deploy step.

Decoupling deployment from release is a powerful way to improve your software delivery process. Not only does it enable you to control the impact of feature release through capabilities such as release targeting and canary releases, but it also reduces risk from failed deployments. Combining the practice of feature management with frequent code merges and deployments reduces the risk of costly merge conflicts and ultimately gets capabilities in front of users faster. These modern deployment practices are necessary to foster high-performing engineering teams and organizations.

Furthermore, they lay the groundwork for optimizing the later stages of the DevOps lifecycle: release, operations, and measurement.

Characteristics of a High-Performance Deployment System

Decoupling the concepts of deployment and release gives us an opportunity to dive into the question, What are the characteristics of a high-performance deployment system? Having deployment systems and processes in place that can sustain and thrive in a continuous model is critical to achieving a state of continuous operations. High-performance deployment systems approach the problem of deployment from a scale perspective, layering in concepts like visibility and orchestration as paths to achieving better scale and deployment velocity.

Visibility lets broader teams see, manage, and interact with system or platform changes. Deployment orchestration moves infrastructure and code changes in concert with each other, often managing adjacent infrastructure or platform dependencies, as well as the ability to deploy previous versions of the workload and upgrade to new versions.

VISIBILITY

An ideal deployment system provides a platform through which you can see what's going out to your workload fleet, manage change, and roll changes back or forward. Visibility provides a wide view into workload deployments, allowing fast response to performance degradation, system errors, or other problems within the environment. Often, automating the deployment process focuses on raw execution of a task and the reduction of human error; however, these tools often fall short of giving you true visibility into the platform. As teams work through operationalizing these functions, they should ensure that their tooling is providing visibility into the state of their workloads. This is not meant to refer to observability tooling explicitly, but it can be included in many cases. Visibility, in the way we discuss it here, refers to a view of the deployment system as a whole.

Visibility becomes increasingly important in environments in which workloads are being delivered automatically (whether by CI/CD or through other types of deployment automation). Quickly understanding when deployments have failed, which workloads are impacted, the rollback status, and the overall impact is critical in reducing not only negative perceptions within end-user communities but also business impacts such as lost revenue and organizational toil.

DEPLOYMENT ORCHESTRATION

Deployment orchestration saves time and reduces errors by removing human interaction not only from the process of deploying software but from adjacent dependencies as well. There are often dependencies within your team processes, other application tooling, or even infrastructure and configurations that need to be included as part of your deployment. Sometimes you need to make changes to the configurations of a database, upgrade server capacity, or phase out other infrastructure components entirely. You may want to include specific technical business logic, such as the inclusion of replica deployments in the strategy or high-availability storage configurations. Orchestration tools build on the concept of automation by coordinating concepts such as these across multiple applications or platforms to help achieve a desired state.

Orchestration helps in two main areas:

Time to deploy to production
Coordinating infrastructure and code changes in tandem can be compli-
cated and fraught with risk. Orchestration allows these processes to move
in concert with each other, thereby reducing order of operations issues and
accelerating speed to production. A good way to think about this is to focus
less on the activity of deployment and more on the time it takes for code to
become usable in a production deployment.

Repeatability
The other goal of orchestration is repeatability. You should be able to
deploy what was live yesterday or last week. Sometimes deployments perform poorly, and you need to roll back to a previously known stable version.
Modern tools allow teams to apply new configurations that will quickly
redeploy or roll back an existing deployment and revert to a version that
they know worked.

Deployment Strategies and Shipping Code

Traditionally, site reliability engineers (SREs) or system admins deployed infrastructural changes and engineers deployed compiled code. To the outside
observer, these roles looked very similar: individuals with the word *engineer* in
their title (usually) who moved software into production. But the practice of
deploying infrastructure evolved separately from the practice of deploying code.

Note

We're using *developer* and *engineer* interchangeably. We understand that some
companies view engineer as a higher-responsibility role than developer. Sometimes
the word *engineer* is what appears in a job title but *developer* is used more collo-
quially. Developers face the same challenges as engineers, so to avoid pulling a
Ballmer and repeating *developer* over and over again, we're using the two terms
interchangeably. It's worth noting that the roles may have different legal or licensing
requirements in specific countries, so be aware.

Working in small batch sizes, collaborating with people in tangential roles,
and testing outcomes have revolutionized software development. Trunk-based
development and the adoption of Git have codified processes around these ideas.

Application teams have been deploying code using A/B tests and canary
deployments in various ways for years. The benefits have been highly visible

to others in technology organizations, and so the ideas began to spread beyond software developers.

In the software realm, these ideas aren't new or revolutionary. What is new is the concept of leveraging these same strategies to drive similar iterations on the underlying infrastructure and supporting platforms. This sharing of ideas, philosophies, and language has enabled both developer and operational teams to work together more cohesively and move faster—and it ultimately forms the foundation of the idea of DevOps: bringing "developer" and "operations" concepts closer to each other.

Let's dive into two infrastructural deployment strategies that have their genesis in software development practices.

BLUE/GREEN DEPLOYMENTS AND CANARIES

Canary deployments and blue/green deployments are both adaptations of software development practices into an operational use case. They allow teams to deploy new application versions safely. Both allow automatic, low-risk deployment to production with the option to roll back easily if necessary. These two deployment strategies are often conflated, leading to the exclusive use of one or the other. But why rely on one? This section covers their use cases and differences so you can use the appropriate one in a given situation. We also cover the supporting constructs of environment copies and targeting.

Understanding blue/green deployments

Blue/green deployments (see *Figure 1-2*) require an exact copy of your entire stack to create two identical versions: a current or "blue" one, and a new or "green" one. Once the new feature is sufficiently tested with a small subset of the total users on the green version, you keep updating to a greater subset of users until all users are routed to the green version. If anything goes wrong, the blue version is still running, and traffic can easily be switched back to the primary running location.

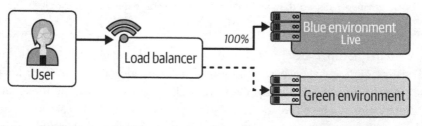

Figure 1-2. Blue/green deployments

Since you are providing an entire copy of your stack, you also need to ensure any necessary data (database content and supporting schemas, for example) or platforms (Kubernetes environments and so on.) exist within both environments to ensure an effective blue/green test. For this effort, you get a strategy that provides an easy fallback to your blue environment if green becomes nonfunctional.

Blue/green deployments necessitate a lot of background work to spin up identical copies of an application software stack. This is still true even in a containerized world, but with a very different set of operational burdens. Do you spin up the identical copies in the same Kubernetes cluster? You also have to manage tagging the workloads differently for the load balancer. In addition, you might have to work with network and DNS teams to manage flipping load balancer targets and weighting around.

When you are ready to make the switch, simply point the router/load balancer/DNS at the green (new) version of the application. If the deployment "event" goes well, the blue version can be spun down or can be kept available so that the router can point the traffic back to the blue version at any point, but in the meantime, traffic will be going to your new version.

Keeping the blue version online gives you more time to see how the green version performs and whether it's achieving the goals you put forward (user adoption, performance changes, etc.), but that ultimately costs money. Maintaining identical environments and databases can be quite expensive. That cost comes in the form of increased cloud provider bills—and that's without considering the salary and opportunity costs of engineers setting up supporting infrastructure or duplicate database schemas/configurations.

Beyond the infrastructure cost of this approach, teams also run against the operational complexity "cost" that arises from managing multiple independent deployments of an application—especially as teams expand workloads into non-traditional platforms such as Kubernetes, serverless, or other managed offerings. Beyond the running infrastructure, there are complexities that arise with adjacent technologies and the teams that manage them. For example, load balancing and DNS technologies are often managed by different teams than the ones who manage traditional infrastructure components; thus, careful coordination between these teams is needed to effectively execute a blue/green deployment when there isn't sufficient automation in place to orchestrate these changes.

Blue/green deployments also suffer complexity in the realm of targeting rules. As mentioned already, the switch between blue and green is typically controlled via an atomic switch, and while there are options to control which version individual users receive, those are typically complex to implement and often rely on dedicated infrastructure configurations to implement successfully.

Understanding canary deployments

The term *canary deployment* comes from when coal miners would bring a bird-cage with a canary inside deep into mines. Canaries have tiny, sensitive lungs, so if the canary dropped dead, it was an early warning to the miners that the air was unsafe.

Just as actual canaries helped coal miners test air quality, canary deployments (see *Figure 1-3*) allow teams to test new infrastructure and reduce the impact scope. When you flip a traffic ingress controller (like NGINX or an AWS load balancer), a canary deployment points a percentage of traffic to the new and old versions of the service at the same time using a load balancer. This enables teams to see how the new version is functioning relative to the old version and allows for a gradual rollout of the new version as confidence increases.

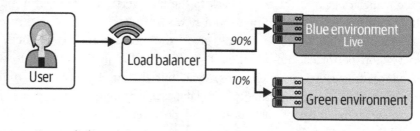

Figure 1-3. Canary deployments

Canary deployments expose a subset of traffic to a new version of a service or application at the load balancer layer. Instead of copying your entire stack, you can copy only the specific components you want to run the canary against and test changes quickly and safely. Canaries are an integral part of a modern deployment cycle, but they aren't always necessary. Evaluate whether or not a change should be canaried against the potential user or system impact. While not all changes need to be run through a canary process, there are many risk reduction benefits to running canaries, especially in higher-impact scenarios.

Leveraging a canary release strategy is often easier because there isn't a need to duplicate wider sets of your application topology. Since you are working only with a specific component, sending traffic to a new version of that component is typically much more approachable.

From a targeting perspective, complexities exist within canary deployments as well. One challenge is the concept of stickiness. Canaries rely on bucketing users to show them one or the other version of the service or application. What happens if a user in the version 1 bucket refreshes the page and then gets assigned version 2? You want to have users "stick" to one version or the other to ensure consistency of experience. At the application level, this situation can be handled easily with a feature flag (see *Chapter 2*) because you know much more about the user context, such as payment history, identity, employer, geography, and so on.

Canaries are frequently executed at the infrastructure level, however, so the point of ingress (load balancer, ingress controller, or some other system allowing inbound connectivity) often doesn't know anything about the user identity. Thus, targeting is much more rudimentary. There are several potential ways to target, such as through geolocation data, IP ranges, and other physical characteristics, but many of these require technical work to orchestrate and offer less granularity than feature flags.

Which should be used?

Blue/green and canary deployments have a lot in common. Each approach can automatically route traffic to new versions of applications, and each provides the ability to roll back quickly and easily to the old default version should issues arise.

The differences lie in what needs to be copied and how much control you have in release targeting. Blue/greens are heavier and blunter, as they require an exact copy of your entire stack and do not allow percentage rollouts. Canaries do not require wider infrastructure or database duplication and do allow granular targeting controls.

Both strategies promote safer deployments but have varying operational or financial implications.

Use a blue/green deployment if:

- The duplication of infrastructure is minimal.
- The operational requirement of the duplication is manageable.
- You are comfortable with moving significant parts of your user community to the new version at the same time.

Use a canary deployment if:

- You are deploying a specific component in your application stack.
- You want the ability to gradually migrate a subset of your users for testing/validation.
- You are embracing feature flags.

DEPLOYING CODE

As with the CI process of writing, building, and testing code, much can be said about code deployment. Books have been written about it, companies have been created, frameworks that address it have become commonplace, and open source ideas have seen wide adoption.

In this section, we offer a high-level overview of a modern code deployment pattern that represents a thoughtful, efficient approach.

After you have committed your code in a Git repository and all code checks have run (through the CI process), your build process system sees that and runs a build command. This compiles the code, injects it into some form of runtime, and places it in an artifact repository. This artifact is then used in the deployment, in which it is shipped into the organization's application environment (the CD portion of the process) and can be released by others closer to the user.

In the legacy model, the end stage of this process would have constituted a release, but with our separation of deployment and release, this is no longer the case. While the new code is deployed out to the infrastructure, feature flags allow code to be selectively targeted at specific user cohorts. Code can be in the production environment while remaining inaccessible to any and all users. In this case, code that has been deployed (placed in an environment) has not necessarily been released—made visible—to users.

One way to think about code deployment is to imagine a clothing boutique that has ordered some dresses via FedEx. Once the dressmaker has made the dresses, it packages them in a box and tells FedEx the shipment is ready. A delivery person comes to the company, picks up the package, and then delivers it to the boutique. If the boutique opens the package and sees that the dresses are torn or are the wrong color, it will take issue with the dressmaker, not FedEx.

Similarly, code deployment takes place after the code has been compiled into a build but before it's been released to the user. And while a giant box with lots of dresses, shoes, purses, and hats is more likely to have some items missing or damaged, a small deployment with only one dress reduces the chance for errors and increases the ability to diagnose the issue.

DORA METRICS (MINUS MTTR)

The DevOps Research and Assessment (DORA) metrics are the best way to measure operational performance. Dr. Nicole Forsgren, Jez Humble, and Gene Kim founded DORA in 2018, and Google acquired the company in 2018. In their groundbreaking 2018 book *Accelerate* (*https://oreil.ly/Bgxuh*) (IT Revolution Press), Forsgren, Humble, and Kim outlined four metrics that have become the gold standard for evaluating software delivery performance:

Change lead time
> The time between when code is committed and when it is pushed to production

Deployment frequency
> How often changes are pushed to production

Change failure rate
> The percentage of changes that fail or cause incidents

Mean time to recovery (MTTR)
> The time between incident declaration and system recovery or incident resolution

These metrics provide ways to quantify, measure, and improve upon facets of building and shipping software. The DORA team isn't the first to define standards with the hope of universal adoption. Other metrics such as lines of code or velocity of stories (small pieces of work in an Agile framework) have been floated as ways to measure software delivery.

Lines of code sounded great from the perspective of nontechnologists, but adding lines of code doesn't necessarily equate to better code. Stripe famously revolutionized the payments industry when it offered developers a way to integrate their payment processing platform by adding only seven lines of code. Quantity of code isn't quality of code.

Story completion velocity was another metric that gained traction. The problem was the lack of standardization of stories. One team could inflate its metrics by breaking down stories into smaller and smaller chunks. Think of this as adding items like "brush my teeth" or "check the mail" to your to-do list so you can give yourself credit for accomplishing a lot that day.

The DORA metrics don't focus on code lines written or stories completed. They measure the health of the software delivery process overall, from when changes get made to when they fail in production. DORA metrics are becoming widely adopted, and technology practitioners owe the DORA team a debt of gratitude for standardizing the field. Sometimes new standards or metrics fail to replace previous versions and lead to even more standards proliferation.

Three of the four DORA metrics are relevant to deployment: change failure rate, deployment frequency, and change lead time. We'll cover those here, and we'll discuss the remaining metric (MTTR) in *Chapter 3, "Operate"*, where it is more relevant.

Note

One could argue that the measurement of any type of metric fits into Chapter 4, "Measure and Experiment". Metrics are a thing you measure, right? As we discuss the transformation of deploy, it makes more sense to include the specific measurement benchmarks that we intend for teams to follow within the current chapter. In Chapter 4 we will dive deeper into the ways teams measure success as they move into a more continuous operating model.

Change lead time

Change lead time measures the time between when code is committed and when it is running in production. If lead times are long, you should examine development or deployment pipelines to identify and remove the bottlenecks.

In a perfect world, the imaginary "change lead time" stopwatch would start at the point that a team selects a feature to begin developing from something like a kanban board, where development tasks are collected, or from the initial user request for a new feature or bug fix. Unfortunately, starting the clock so far back introduces a lot of variability that makes the metric less useful. What if a feature is selected just before a major holiday, or before a high-severity incident? Time can tick by (in software development as in life!) and inflate the metric without it meaningfully measuring the work. Starting the measurement when code is committed simplifies the metric and makes it more of an apples-to-apples comparison.

Every year the DORA team surveys the software development industry and publishes its seminal State of DevOps report. In the 2022 report (*https://oreil.ly/9wqLJ*) (the most recent one at the time of writing), the DORA team says that low-performing teams have change lead times between one and six months, medium-performing teams are between one week and one month, and high-performing teams are between one day and one week.

Testing often takes up a large chunk of the change lead time. If you want to improve your results on this metric, automate testing practices as much as possible to lower the time necessary for changes. Having engineers run automated tests when they are writing code, or instituting automatic testing procedures as part of the code check-in process, can lower this metric tremendously.

Deployment frequency

Deployment frequency refers to the volume of deployments to production over a set period of time. This is often the easiest of the DORA metrics to measure, and it is the one that is most likely to be measured currently or to have been measured previously. The goal of any company's technology team is to deliver value to its customers as often as possible, with as little disruption as possible. Deployment frequency intuitively seems to measure that—more deployments equals more responsiveness. But this metric actually measures something else.

As touched on earlier in this chapter, deployment frequency has a direct influence on the volume of code changes within a commit or the size of the change set and on the frequency of code merges. The deployment frequency will inherently be low if teams have large batch sizes. Large batch sizes with infrequent merges run a higher risk of creating merge conflicts. If there are many changes in a batch, they all must work together, and sorting out merge conflicts takes time, reducing the frequency at which deployments can happen. Inversely, if teams have small batch sizes and deployments change individually, there is less potential for merge conflicts, removing one of the most common barriers to shipping newly developed code continuously.

The 2022 State of DevOps report defined low performers as those who deployed between once a month and once every six months, medium performers as deploying between once a week and once a month, and high performers as deploying on demand multiple times per day.

To increase deployment frequency, keep branch time short, reduce batch sizes, and merge code into main more often. The more frequently code is brought into your deployment trunk, the more frequently it can be compiled and shipped out to your user communities for consumption.

Change failure rate

Change failure rate is the percentage of changes that result in incidents or failures. The previous two metrics measure the tempo and quantity of changes pushed to production, while this one measures the *quality* of changes. The result will be poor if quantity and speed are high but the quality is low.

This metric defines quality as not causing an incident. Measuring changes can be squishy. Do you look at utilization? Product teams awaiting a big announcement can block some changes from release. Users will engage with some changes ("new sign-in page") more than others ("Danish language support now available"). Since evaluating the quality of changes is so fraught, a more standard bar is necessary. Not causing an incident is fair and easy to measure, so it's a useful stand-in for "change quality."

The 2022 report indicated that low performers experienced a failure rate of 46%–60%, medium performers were between 16% and 30%, and high performers had a failure rate between 0% and 15%.

An important distinction to make is between change failure rate and the number of change failures. In real-world scenarios, change failures are going to happen, even with the best planning. It's much more realistic to manage the rate at which these change failures occur to understand trending, and to work to manage severity and recoverability. Organizations that have embraced the "smaller change/deploy more often" operating posture are likely to have incidents that are easier to debug and quicker to record due to more manageable change sets.

Summary

Deploying code transforms letters, numbers, and symbols into business value. Establishing stronger, high-performing deployment systems and practices accelerates the pace of achieving that business value. These systems reduce the chance of error by providing better visibility and orchestration across your deployment environments.

Deploy used to mean something akin to "make available." This made sense in an age when software came on CDs in boxes. With the ubiquity of the cloud, a faster, more ever-present delivery model is available. The actual mechanics of pressing CDs no longer constrains deployments.

Deployment often flies under the radar unless it breaks down. Deployment efficiency (speed of the actual deployment, for example) isn't a user-facing concept. Users experience the downstream impacts of when software is deployed. This includes concepts such as outages, or new features being made available.

Adopting a delivery posture that commits smaller code, merges that code, and deploys more frequently helps create a user environment that is moving forward continuously.

Deployment failures will happen regardless. Leveraging strategies such as blue/green deployments and canaries gives teams a greater ability to mitigate the risk of these failures impacting actual users. Moving a step further, using feature flags to break apart the deploy step from the release step gives even greater control over risk and user experience. All these concepts together enable teams to deploy software more quickly to end users.

2

Release

Now that we have a firm understanding of deployment strategies, let's look more closely at the next stage of the improved framework, *release* (see *Figure 2-1*). This is perhaps the most exciting and impactful stage because it represents when users, or the people most commonly consuming the software or features being released, are able to see and adopt new functionality within their application. For these same individuals, the deploy and measure stages are (hopefully) invisible. The operate stage focuses on the ongoing "care and feeding" of the application and its underlying platform, including when things go wrong. Release represents the big reveal!

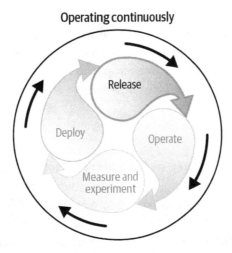

Figure 2-1. The release stage

As discussed in *Chapter 1*, the modernized framework reverses the position of deploy and release. Deploy is the first step of the ops process, in which code is placed in a software environment. After code has been deployed, the various features enabled within its deployment are ready to be released for consumption.

The release process has undergone a significant shift in orthodoxy in recent years, and not just because it's the most outwardly visible segment. New tools, ideas, and processes—particularly feature flags and the feature management systems that operate them—have fundamentally transformed the way teams release changes to their applications.

Feature flagging represents a significant component of this transformation. Feature flags themselves are a simple idea to implement. They are enormously powerful, especially when adopted as a foundational development practice for controlling user experience and managing risk.

The term *feature flag* is based on the idea that a feature, or subset of code, is toggled on or off by using a configuration object—in this case, a flag. The flag itself, while part of the code, is not part of the actual feature; it is simply the mechanism that controls whether a given feature is enabled or disabled. Feature management builds on this concept by providing a scalable practice of configuring these flags across teams and users, enabling different feature flag types as well as the ability to use targeting to influence the user experience and configurations of applications.

How do feature flags become a critical part of the modern release process? Who releases software, to whom is it released, and when? How frequent are releases? What strategies can be used to optimize performance? This chapter will answer these questions and explore how release stands alone as a core part of operating continuously.

Feature Flags

Feature flags (or *toggles*, as they are sometimes called) allow developers to display code changes to specific users without having to redeploy. They can be simple and straightforward or deep and powerful, depending on how sophisticated the developer wants the implementation to be. As discussed in *Chapter 1*, feature management can be used for feature validation, canary releases, risk mitigation, A/B/n testing, personalization, entitlements, and more. More broadly, it is a key component in decomposing larger applications into a more manageable state for rapid and safe development. Borrowing an example from the infrastructure space, there is a strong parallel to the concept of "transitioning a monolith into microservices"—where you take an existing application and break up its functionality into multiple microservices that can be independently managed.

In the case of a larger codebase, feature flagging provides development teams better flexibility around developing features independently of other application components. This separation creates a better developer experience and a more manageable system overall. Furthermore, this allows the application deployment, release, feature, or integration to exist as discrete chunks that can be turned on or off for specific users or teams at specific times. Feature flags can also be used as workflow enforcement mechanisms, moving code from developer to reviewer to production. To better understand their use cases, let's look at what feature flags are and how they work.

The most basic implementations of feature flags are Boolean if/else statements within the application code. These types of flags control whether code executes (and is presented to users). For example, if a flag that controls beta access is "on," users will see the beta version; if the flag is "off," users will see the default version:

```
if(app_settings["beta-mode"] == "true")
  showbeta();
else
  existing();
```

In feature management, this concept extends to user targeting, in which you target users, groups of users, or other configurable parameters with specific feature flag values—creating for them a very different experience from that of other users.

However, framing the concept of feature flags around the simplicity of an if/else statement can be misleading. At first glance, this can seem basic and humdrum: it's just an if/else statement, so what's the big deal? If a user is in California, show them the CCPA notice. If not, don't. Pretty simple, right?

To truly appreciate the capabilities feature flags enable, we need to think much bigger. Consider the use case of rolling out software, or a change across a global footprint. By leveraging the combination of feature flagging and targeting rules (see *Chapter 1*), you can have limitless options for creating a fine-grained rollout. Maybe you want to roll this change out by time zone, allowing it to take place regionally at the earliest hours, to reduce the risk of a failed deployment or the impact on user teams. Historically, this practice would be gated behind complex technology implementations such as special DNS configurations, load balancers, or geographic weighting. Implementing these in a manner that truly solves the problem would be a costly burden from both the operational and supporting infrastructure standpoints.

Alternatively, what if you want to enable self-service opt-in to this new capability, while still presenting the existing, unchanged application to all other users? Maybe you want to expose this to your development team as well. What if you run into a problem with these targeted user groups and you need the change disabled? Using feature flags to manage the release of features, decoupled from the deployment, makes all these achievements possible.

We cover deployment in greater detail in *Chapter 1*. However, feature flags allow this decoupling by providing a way to have a feature removed from user interaction until you are ready for users to consume it. Teams can execute the deployment of their software, validate that the deployment (i.e., moving the application code to a specified environment) was successful, and—once they have that validation—release the feature by enabling it and configuring whom it is targeted at. We will cover release targeting in greater detail later in this chapter.

While feature flags are instrumented within the application code, the optimal case has them being managed using a feature flag management tool. Unlike with blue/green and canary deployments, no copies of infrastructure, databases, or complete stacks need to be created or maintained to use a feature flag. Many teams are already using tooling similar to feature flags within their code to conditionally execute parts of their application. As they expand this practice to adopt concepts such as user targeting, the complexities of instrumenting their own flag management system become more apparent.

Building a feature management system from scratch represents a significant technical and operational burden. Humans make mistakes and thus try to remove human error as a potential cause of failure. Many open source and SaaS feature management solutions offer the benefits of feature flags without the risk of an errant keystroke. These tools typically work by installing software development kits (SDKs) for relevant programming languages and controlling feature flags through a SaaS UI or via the API.

The Power of Feature Flags

Feature flags are tools. As noted earlier, at their most basic level they let you turn features on and off.

The true superpower of feature flags becomes immediately apparent in the ability to target releases granularly. The once-heretical idea of testing new software deployments and their features in production becomes possible since new code can be hidden from most users behind a feature flag and disabled (toggled off) quickly in the event of a problem. We'll explore this testing concept more later in this chapter. Entitlements can be enforced, so users see the features they are supposed to see. Beyond tier-level entitlements, personalization options unfurl, as feature flags are the mechanism by which companies are able to target changes, based on user data they already have, to create more relevant and positive experiences within the application. We'll discuss these concepts in this section.

GRANULAR TARGETING

Feature flags are so powerful because they allow extremely granular targeting. Blue/green and canary deployments offer only rudimentary targeting with the trade-off of higher complexity, but feature flags offer targeting down to identifying attributes like user IDs. Blue/greens and canaries work at the infrastructure layer, which has no insight into individual user attributes. Feature flags work within the application layer. They can interact at a user and service level—leveraging more identifiers tied to the consumers of the services.

For example, account ID is commonly used in business-to-business (B2B) contexts in which distinct customers have access to certain features and usage limits. Location can be used to offer locally relevant information or create a geographically bounded beta group. User device information can be used to target features at specific devices for testing out a new mobile configuration. Pricing tiers can be used to add new features to users based on how much they pay. Ecommerce companies can use purchase history or shopping cart amounts to offer discounts or special offers. Internal employees can be shown early versions of changes to act as an alpha group.

The most advanced feature flagging platforms allow teams to target based on more than just user identity characteristics. Teams can leverage the region being connected from (such as US-West), device type, operating system, or any other identifiable characteristics. The possibilities are endless.

PROGRESSIVE DELIVERY

Progressive delivery is the practice of gradually releasing software changes into an environment. Software is delivered to controlled groups of individuals, and the distribution of the release is gradually increased as success criteria are met—or the release is rolled back as problems arise. The practice gives organizations a path to implementing continuous delivery in production environments with manageable risk. Understanding progressive delivery and how it can be implemented lets teams release code faster and more safely and opens the door for foundational DevOps use cases.

Continuous delivery is a set of practices that ensure your code is always in a deployable state by increasing the frequency at which code is committed, built, tested, and deployed. In the past, these steps occurred only at the end of a project, when it was "code complete."

Progressive delivery has two main tenets:

Release progression

The technique of first delivering changes to small, low-risk audiences and then expanding to larger and riskier audiences, validating the results as you go

Delegation progression

The progressive delegation of the feature's control to the owner most closely responsible for the outcome

Since you cannot achieve progressive delivery without modern release practices, it is critical to understand how to transform a release management process into progressive delivery.

Release progression

Release progression is the idea that you initially release to a small, trusted group and continually expand to larger, less trusted groups. This concept is intuitive, as it reflects how people act in the real world. If someone is contemplating a drastic change to a relationship or job, they don't broadcast their thoughts to everyone immediately. They typically seek guidance from trusted friends and family so they can learn how their reasoning sounds to a sympathetic third party. From there they might discuss the idea more widely or, if they decide against it, stop discussing it completely.

Note

This is also called a *canary release*, which is similar in concept to a canary deployment. Instead of deploying infrastructure to an increasingly widening percentage of traffic, code is released to an increasing percentage of users. To avoid confusion, we use *canaries* to refer to canary deployments and *release progression* to refer to canary releases.

This is analogous to release progression. Software is complex, and changes do not always achieve the desired outcome. Releasing a change to a close-knit group of people, perhaps other developers at your company, provides two benefits: a high likelihood of friendly feedback, and minimal impact of negative consequences.

The initial batch, or ring, of users to try a new feature should be very trust-worthy. This group can be internal employees, contributors to an open source project, or users who have opted into early access programs. You need to be able to rely upon them to offer honest, constructive feedback. This feedback should inform the decision of whether to roll out to a wider audience or roll back the release for further tuning.

Negative feedback, whether acquired manually from alpha users or automat-ically from observability tools, should be treated with respect. Whatever isn't working for a small number of users or systems would likely have a much larger impact on a larger release audience. So releasing early versions to small groups minimizes the risk of releasing new software and removes one of the barriers to a faster release cycle.

If the change has been released to a small group of users and the feedback has been nominal or positive, you should release it to a wider audience. If you started with internal users, a logical next step might be to expand to those users who opted into the early access program, to beta customers, or perhaps to a particular customer group that has been requesting the change. You can also begin releasing to a small percentage of your overall user community or to users in a geographic area distant from the majority of users.

Just as before, let the human and automatic feedback guide the decision to release more widely or to stop and iterate on the change. The feedback will help you deliver software your users actually want, since they will tell you whether or not the change accomplishes its task. Furthermore, companies are constantly trying to deliver value to their customers; the faster they hear and can iterate on feedback, the faster they will deliver products and services that customers want. Release stage length can vary from organization to organization, and it's extremely challenging to estimate within this book, but most commonly these release cycles play out within a time frame of weeks.

Release progression is a transformative concept that is being successfully implemented at several large companies already. The following examples of release progression (or progressive delivery) illustrate its advantages.

Netflix uses geographic release progressions to test pricing changes (*https:// oreil.ly/5_orx*). For years, Netflix allowed users to share passwords. When the company's stock price tumbled in the spring of 2022, it decided to test various types of password-sharing restrictions to see which of them increased revenue without generating an equivalent amount of customer churn. Netflix decided to test two options: charging subscribers to add users to their account for an additional fee, and charging users to add homes to an account. It tested the former option in Peru, Chile, and Costa Rica and the latter in Argentina and Honduras. By running the tests in different countries, Netflix was able to have large enough sample sizes to increase its confidence that the results were representative of what might occur if either test were rolled out more widely.

Hawaiian Airlines used release progression to improve responsiveness at the start of the COVID-19 pandemic (*https://oreil.ly/ZLovS*). When COVID hit, the airline industry was thrust into chaos. Airlines, including Hawaiian, experienced huge cancellations, and customer support inquiries spiked. Before COVID, customers couldn't cancel or rebook their flights themselves. When the cancellation onslaught swamped its customer support team, Hawaiian rolled out a way for customers to handle these requests themselves. It released the new functionality to a small subset of customers, gradually increasing the rollout percentage as its confidence grew in the new service. Without release progression, Hawaiian wouldn't have been able to roll out such timely changes so quickly.

Delegation progression

Just as release progression allows for a continual widening of the audience for a software change, delegation progression allows for a transfer of ownership to those most closely responsible for the outcome. It also offers a more enterprise-friendly use case for testing in production.

Delegation progression means engineers can pass the baton of release ownership to product owners early in the process, allowing the engineers to focus more on developing code, while product owners manage feature release and targeting configurations. Incomplete code can be deployed to production and delegated to product owners. Being closer to the users in most cases, product owners have more insight into release groups and cadences. They are the main audience and beneficiaries of the feedback that alpha and beta users provide, so it makes sense for them to receive the feedback without intermediaries. They can toggle the feature flags that control the release and run their own experiments and beta groups.

As we've mentioned, delegation progression also frees up developers to focus on code development instead of feature releasing. The incomplete code that was shipped in the previous example can continue to be worked on, while product teams enable aspects of the new feature for early testing by end users. Once new code is feature complete, product owners who have been delegated control continue to manage the release process while engineering and developer teams move on to their next development tasks. Since the product owners will handle the release, the engineers' time that would otherwise be allocated to the release can be spent on the next sprint.

Delegation progression gives the engineer and the product owner more time to focus on the core functionality of their respective roles. Both will be happier and more productive as a result.

Feature flags generally make the most sense for delegation progressions. Individuals outside of operations can operate a feature flag easily. And as there is no infrastructure to copy, the effort in standing up a feature flag is much lower than that associated with other deployment techniques.

TESTING IN PRODUCTION

Testing in production sounds stressful and amazing at the same time. No matter how much you try, your staging environment is inevitably different from production. What works in staging might not work in production. Testing in production offers the opportunity to try out software changes the way your users might experience them.

Another benefit of testing in production is the opportunity to have fewer testing environments. Environments are expensive to maintain but are necessary for testing. If some of the testing can be safely done in production, then the need and cost justification for staging environments are diminished.

However, a *lot* of caution is necessary here. *Testing in production* is a pretty loaded term. The whole point of environments like dev, testing, and staging is to safely test features out of sight of users. Many companies, especially larger enterprises, spend enormous amounts of time and resources architecting a system of workflows and approvals to prohibit or limit testing in production. They make sure that any change to a production environment has been checked and rechecked before it is exposed to users.

Granted, these approval processes were usually put in place before the practices of feature flags and testing in production gained mindshare and popularity. But the point remains that enterprises are allergic to risk, and testing in production seems to circumvent a lot of guardrails and change management designed specifically to minimize risk.

Despite the resistance to risk in large organizations, there are still benefits to testing in production—more accurate test results thanks to a presumably larger user pool, for example, as well as better feedback from observability tools. Nevertheless, forward-thinking leaders at larger enterprises who are trying to implement a practice of testing in production might run into more organizational resistance than would their counterparts at smaller companies. Leveraging feature management gives organizations the ability to limit their blast radius if an issue arises in the environment by controlling access to the feature being tested, thus mitigating some of this risk while still gaining the benefits we mentioned previously.

The best place to test is where the people already are. No matter how hard you try, staging will never equal production in terms of volume and complexity. This is why the "Well, it worked in staging" joke is so widely used. Changes can work in testing environments but perform differently in production. Testing in production increases accuracy.

Testing in production also provides the ability to enable access to a platform for your team even while it's down for others. When there is an incident in production, every second counts. Releasing a fix to the entire user community has significant risk associated with it. Feature flags allow potential fixes to be tested in the production environment, targeted at users you can validate success with directly. This gives confidence that the potential fix solves the problem and is ready to be released more widely. By expediting the incident remediation process, feature flags decrease incident duration. (We'll cover incidents in depth in *Chapter 4*.)

At more nimble organizations, testing in production enables teams to gain traction quickly. Anyone using a small service understands (hopefully) that the price to pay for transformation technology is occasionally tolerating bugs or degraded usability. Enterprise workflows can slow down the development, deployment, and releasing of new software, so nimble startups can compete on speed. Testing in production and bypassing time-consuming change management processes gives startups an advantage over more well-known, better-resourced enterprises.

Since feature flags allow the deployment of code into production while keeping the execution of that code disabled for customers, software can be safely deployed to production and tests can be run to see how it functions in the real world. Other deployment strategies do not allow such targeted flexibility.

Testing in production is impossible without feature flags. In a world where deploy and release are tied together, there is no way to test in production with a small group of users. A test would have to go out to all users, and the developers wouldn't have a way to incorporate the learnings of the test until the next deploy.

PERSONALIZATION

With feature flags, developers can provide personalized experiences to users, using what they know about the users to provide more valuable interactions. Users can vary widely across a variety of categories: geographic, demographic, source of traffic, device, browser, language, and so on. Companies go to great lengths to understand their user base because they want to continually offer users what they want. The more a company knows about its users, the easier it will be to predict and build what they want.

Note

At first glance, personalization seems a lot like granular targeting. They are manifestations of the same idea: using data about users to give them different experiences. Personalization is the use of granular targets as a mechanism for customizing the user experience based on specific data. It refers to frontend optionality based on knowledge of a user—if someone bought a beach towel and sand toys, for example, suggest they buy sunscreen as well. Granular targeting can be for frontend changes or backend systems like APIs or what regional database is being consumed by a given user or group. Perhaps a social media company wants to have different backend configurations for all accounts with a follower count above a certain threshold. That's an example of granular targeting, but not of personalization.

There are many frontend examples of useful personalization. Clothing brands can display warmer clothes for users in cold climates. Streaming companies can display movies and content that similar users have watched. Pet food companies can offer products aimed at the animals the user owns. For business-to-consumer (B2C) companies in particular, the importance of personalization is hard to overstate.

Feature flags are the vehicle that allows the utilization of user data. Rental car companies can create feature flags that say: if a user is looking for a rental car in Hawaii, Los Angeles, or Las Vegas, highlight convertibles; or if the user is looking for a rental car in Alaska, Colorado, or Montana, offer all-wheel-drive vehicles. The same rental car company can offer a unique experience to users in different places.

One of the less discussed but more interesting things about feature flags is how they democratize control over the user experience. Without them, changes that impact users need to be made by developers or people who can work directly with the codebase. Developers need to implement feature flags, but once those are created, product managers, marketers, customer success managers, and more can use them to show different variations to subsections of users. As long as those other personas understand how the data is structured, they can manipulate what users see without asking engineers to make their changes.

One way to increase the velocity or throughput of your product delivery team is to remove the bottlenecks each role faces. Marketing, product, and growth teams have lots of personalization ideas. Empowering them with feature flags allows them to do their jobs without having to ask engineers to implement their plans every single time. This is a double win: teams closer to the user can experiment and iterate faster than if they were bottlenecked developers, and those developers have one less task on their plate.

ENTITLEMENTS

Entitlements define the right to access software applications or certain features. Entitlements can be similar to the targeting that we've talked about in previous discussions, but they're often used as a core feature of your application. They are typically employed to give users features based on their pricing tier—for example, free users get x features, professional plan users get $x + y$, enterprise users get $x + y + z$. This is a very common use case, and feature flags are a mechanism for delivering this functionality.

Entitlements aren't just useful for gating features by pricing tier. Entitlement use cases are very important for highly regulated industries. Laws and regulations vary across states and countries, and software companies need to make sure that they comply. Feature flags allow companies to show or hide functionality to users based on pricing tier, geographic location, or any other factor. They can also help with internationalization by ensuring that users abide by jurisdictional laws.

For example, a European luxury car manufacturer uses feature flags in this manner. The carmaker's mobile app enables users to temporarily give car access to a friend. Some countries don't allow this feature for privacy reasons. The app can detect a user's location by the cell tower it is pinging, and if the cell tower is in a country that allows the car sharing feature, that part of the app shows up. If the app detects that the user is in a country where the feature is prohibited, that part of the app isn't shown.

Feature Management Platforms

Feature flags can exist outside of dedicated feature management platforms. They are often free: you simply edit a configuration file or add a Boolean statement into your codebase. This can work temporarily so long as the person adding the feature flags is on the team and can keep track of them as they proliferate. But what happens when that person or group of people leaves the team? Or what if the team decides to use a different programming language? Or someone makes a typo while editing the configuration code and the team wants to remove the offending code without a redeployment? What if the team wants to use an external system to manage the way it targets changes at users?

Feature management platforms allow organizations to manage their feature flags and experiments at scale. There are many offerings out there (including LaunchDarkly) that serve a wide array of use cases. Make sure that the feature management system you choose meets your needs (and those of your customers) both today and in the future. A state-of-the-art feature management platform will allow speedy flag delivery, experimentation built on top of feature flags, security, compliance, reliability, delegation progression, flag management, and language support.

SPEED

Consistency and speed matter. Users expect to see the same functionality as their friends and coworkers. The impact of consistency and speed depends on your application. If you sell remote sensors that measure reservoir depth and broadcast levels to agricultural systems every hour, the need for consistent and quick flag rule evaluation (the conditional statements that are applied to a feature flag resolution) is minimal. If you have a high volume of users accessing a consumer application via mobile devices all around the world, your tolerance for uneven or slow flag delivery will be different.

Consistency—polling versus streaming

A feature flag management system needs to do what it says on the box quickly, and without friction. Once a flag is flipped on, the user needs to see the update. Basic feature management systems will use a polling mechanism to deliver flag updates—they check back to a central system and process the updates. The polling mechanism can be set to varying intervals, such as every second, every minute, every five minutes, and so on. These systems are easy to build and thus cost less than premium offerings. The trade-off is product consistency versus efficiency.

You can set the polling frequency to a very short interval, which in most cases will result in the feature management platform constantly pinging your system. This can lead to problems such as battery performance issues for mobile users and increased cost due to frequent connections back to your central systems. Think of these downsides as the technical equivalent of your kids asking "Are we there yet?" over and over again.

A long interval, on the other hand, reduces the chance of battery drain and server cost but decreases UI consistency. Some users see the new update immediately, while others have to wait until the next poll. How many seconds or minutes you can tolerate having different users see different versions is up to you.

Top-of-the-line feature management systems use a streaming architecture in which updates are delivered to the endpoints as the changes are made within the feature management system. Instead of high or low frequency pings for updates, streaming systems broadcast only when there is a change to the flag rules, and the update goes out to all devices at the same time. This approach eliminates the downsides of the polling system regardless of polling frequency. To continue our previous analogy, instead of your kids constantly asking "Are we there yet?" they can be asleep, and you simply wake them up when you've arrived. This streaming connection is often a long-lived one from the application back to the feature management platform.

The most sophisticated systems will leverage streaming when a user is active within the application (browsing, clicking, watching), and fall back to long polling when the application is not active. This conserves battery life and data connectivity and provides a high-quality experience when the application is actively being used.

The importance of a CDN

Distributed is the new normal. Establishing a consistent experience whether someone is connecting from a coffee shop in London or from their office in Oakland is critical. This type of global reach is an expectation of most modern application architectures. State-of-the-art systems use a global content delivery network (CDN) to extend the reach of feature management to meet this global need. CDNs are globally distributed points of presence (in many cases, data centers) that act as a connectivity point, or caching point, to decrease load times and latency for users who might be far from where your service is hosted. In the case of feature management, these provide a closer point of presence to your end users' connectivity, ensuring that your users receive the feature releases (or kill switches) you initiate quickly and consistently. If your users are all close enough in proximity to Virginia, home of AWS US-East-1, then you might be fine without a CDN. But keep in mind that while *you* may not have many users in Perth, your customers might. If your users have a global reach, make sure your feature management system uses a CDN or other edge-aware technologies to deliver consistent updates to users around the world.

EXPERIMENTATION

As teams embrace feature management as a practice, the logical next step is to measure the effectiveness of the features that are being released to users. This entails understanding whether the features are successfully meeting the goals that your organization has established, or testing a hypothesis you might have around the way your system is being consumed. This practice is referred to as *experimentation*. We cover experimentation in great detail in *Chapter 4, "Measure and Experiment"*, so we won't go into it too much here, but any time you are building new features and functionality into an application, it's important to be able to leverage data to understand whether a newly developed feature is meeting the needs of the business. Experimentation allows teams to make data-informed decisions around feature releases. Any feature flag can be an experiment, as the outcomes can be measured and compared for users who are shown any variation. Combining the feature flags you're building with features you want to run experiments on is the fastest way to understand the success and manage the risk of features you are developing. If your team is interested in the practice of experimentation within your applications, look for a feature management system that can do both.

SECURITY

Feature management systems place new code into your codebase and allow control over which code is executed. Choosing a system means granting intimate access to your intellectual property. When you're implementing concepts such as release targeting, feature management SDKs are likely leveraging properties from each user's data or their identity to allow you to use those items to target. These properties might be their office location, their time zone, or even aspects of their connecting device. To minimize the risk associated with giving a third-party access to your code, make sure the feature management system you choose has a robust security process that protects not just the ways that user data is accessed but also the targeting logic itself. Look for vendors that undergo independent penetration testing every six months. Ask them about their security procedures and policies. See if they support your identity provider so you can easily grant and revoke access to the right employees on your team. Your feature management system should encrypt your data both at rest and in transit.

RELIABILITY

Users expect reliability. They need to know that your service will work as expected all the time. Creating software is inherently challenging, and adding a feature management system adds another dependency. The flags that are created in a feature management platform are intricately tied to your codebase. If your feature management system suffers an outage, it might affect your ability to deliver your service.

B2C companies face online scorn that can damage their reputation beyond their users. B2B companies can face the same, and they might owe service credits to their enterprise customers.

Look at a feature management system's status page to see historical downtime. Find out how many nines of uptime the vendor guarantees to see whether it aligns with what you have promised your users. Three nines (99.9% guaranteed uptime) are standard, but some customers demand four (99.99%) or more nines. This will be spelled out in the service-level agreement (SLA). There might be multiple SLAs available at different pricing tiers, with more nines and guarantees of service credits available on enterprise-level service agreements. If your customers demand uptime guarantees from you, you need to demand the same of your feature management system.

COMPLIANCE

If your product doesn't touch or sell to highly regulated industries, you can probably get by with a basic feature management system. Service Organization Control 2 (SOC 2) compliance is one of the most common features of any enterprise pricing plan. If you don't need that, low-cost feature management systems will work.

If you serve highly regulated customers or prospects, talk to them. They will tell you which frameworks you need to comply with to earn their business. Here are some common frameworks that might be relevant; if your customers require your company to comply with any of these, then your feature management system likely needs to comply as well:

SOC 2
> If you touch customer data

Health Insurance Portability and Accountability Act (HIPAA)
> If you work in health care

General Data Protection Regulation (GDPR)
> If any of your customers are in the EU

California Consumer Privacy Act (CCPA)
> If you serve California residents and have more than $25 million in revenue

Federal Risk and Authorization Management Program (FedRAMP)
> If you sell to the US government

There are other frameworks as well. Since your feature management system will be intricately tied to your code and data streams, make sure you choose a system that complies with the frameworks your customers need.

DELEGATION PROGRESSION

We talked about delegation progression at greater length earlier in this chapter, so we will be brief here. Delegation progression allows an engineer to pass the responsibility of releasing code to a teammate who is closer to the user. A feature management system should be usable not just by the engineers who set up the feature flags but also by the product managers, who are more attuned to a feature's reception or performance.

FLAG MANAGEMENT

Feature flags can add a layer of complexity to application code. Some feature flags are permanent (if a user is in California, show the CCPA notice; if not, don't), but some are temporary. Feature flags that roll out features are unnecessary once the feature has been rolled out to 100% of users. If they are not removed, these feature flags can confuse future engineers, making them wonder which feature a flag is for and whether it's safe to remove it. With enough buildup, code cluttered with unused feature flags can have performance issues.

A highlight of strong feature management systems is the availability of tools for minimizing this complexity and managing the lifecycle of feature flags. An example would be capabilities for highlighting unused flags and showing where they are in the codebase. This allows you to have a quicker understanding of how your code is impacted by these flags and to safely remove those that are no longer necessary, eliminating a source of potential complexity and technical debt.

LANGUAGES

Feature management systems connect with their customers' codebases by using SDKs. An SDK will connect to a feature management system's server and return the feature flags. SDKs are language specific.

A common reason for teams outgrowing homegrown solutions is language switching. A homegrown feature flag system might be written in the language(s) used by the team today. If the team decides to use a new language in the future, the existing system becomes obsolete.

When choosing a feature management system, look at the supported SDKs and make sure the vendor has SDKs both for the language(s) you use now and for any languages under consideration for future use.

WORKFLOW ENHANCEMENTS

Your team has established workflows. Code goes along a certain path of environments before reaching production, and some changes need to be approved by people in specific roles. Some feature management systems have tools to support your process. They can schedule flags to be released at a future date and time. Some can map to your approval process to ensure that flags are released only after the appropriate oversight.

Summary

We've expended significant effort throughout this chapter to highlight the power of feature flags. One thing we didn't spend a lot of time on was the idea that once you start developing software in this way, it's very hard to imagine going back to a life without them.

Feature flags are a transformative development tool. Yes, they can be simple, binary if/else statements. But by using them to decouple deploy from release, they open up new possibilities previously thought impossible or heretical.

With feature flagging, features can be released (or blocked) at extremely granular levels, based on whatever data you have on your users. This allows for personalization and entitlements. Personalization gives teams the ability to target experiences at the user level based on what is known about the users. Entitlements grant teams the ability to stay in compliance with local regulation and to ensure users access the right set of features.

Feature flags also enable the twin tenets of progressive delivery: release progression and delegation progression. Software releases are no longer binary. Features can be released to percentages of users and tested before being rolled out more widely. The irony here is that a tool sometimes dismissed for its simplistic, binary nature ended up breaking the binariness of the field of software delivery.

Feature management systems help teams operate and harness the power of feature flags. They offer a wide variety of features and support; choose one that makes sense for your organization now and as you grow.

3

Operate

In the days of shipping software on CDs, software releases were considered done once the CDs were in the users' hands. Now, with software delivered digitally through the cloud or hosted remotely, there isn't an equivalent sense of "done." Complexity abounds and entropy encroaches. The interplay among your code, user behavior, third-party integrations, internal tooling, cloud hosting, and SaaS vendors means that your software can perform unexpectedly at any time. While the previous two chapters focused on deploying changes and releasing software, this next stage in our revised operating continuously model, *operate* (see *Figure 3-1*), is focused on managing the impact of these changes as new features are released into your application landscape.

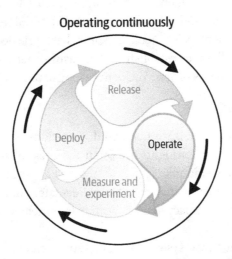

Figure 3-1. The operate stage

While operations are not exclusively about managing incidents, incident management is a critical piece of getting operations running correctly. When incidents aren't handled well, your operations team may find it has little time for anything else. Thus our focus for this chapter will be on identifying and managing incidents.

There are two aspects to dealing with the inevitability of incidents. The first involves what you do before an incident occurs, since one *will* occur. The second is how you handle an incident after it happens.

Before an incident occurs, you want to create processes that limit the impact of that incident on your application, its users, and your organization. In this chapter, we'll discuss some strategies to help you and your team proactively shorten the length of incidents and reduce or eliminate the damage they may cause.

During an incident, you need strategies for identifying the problem, creating a fix, testing that fix, and eventually releasing the fix. Since incident responses require the involvement of technical and/or other staff that can identify and respond to incidents, we'll discuss topics of people management and culture and cover tools that can help improve your response processes.

When reviewing an incident, it is always valuable to reflect on what happened and how well you and your team responded and determine whether any areas need improvement. We'll look at some best practices for post-incident retrospectives and at how to establish and measure metrics that can help you determine the effectiveness of your incident response processes.

What Is an Incident?

As we've already noted, when we talk about operations, we are not just talking about incidents. However, incidents are often the most obvious indicator of the health of your overall operations.

An incident is any event that requires immediate, out-of-band remediation. Urgency and customer impact should be the barometers for determining the severity of an incident.

Incidents are not just system outages. An incident can and should be declared if there is a problem in your system that could lead to an outage, degrade performance, or even prevent access to application functionality, regardless of whether customers are currently unaffected. This is an essential shift toward a proactive incident management process that can detect and mitigate incidents before customers are even aware of them.

Common Incident Causes

Incidents typically have one of three causes:

- Changes to your system
- Changes to the inputs of your system
- Nonsoftware issues

CHANGES TO YOUR SYSTEM

Almost any software system is in a fairly constant state of change—from infrastructure changes, which can include both hardware and software updates, to new features built and deployed by your development team. Any of these changes or updates may cause an incident. In fact, according to *The Visible Ops Handbook* (*https://oreil.ly/fjgko*) by Kevin Behr, Gene Kim, and George Spafford (Information Technology Process Institute), "80% of unplanned outages are due to ill-planned changes made by administrators ('operations staff') or developers."

When it comes to the software we build, continuous deployment makes life easier. Deploying multiple times per day ensures that each individual change will be minor in size and importance. If part of your application starts failing, the most recently released changes are the most obvious culprits. Smaller deployments and releases make rollbacks or kill switches easier, which means easier incident management. (We'll discuss rollbacks and kill switches later in this chapter.) Each release has less complexity to untangle and a narrower scope.

However, frequent updates and deployments, even in small batch sizes, can lead to a higher likelihood of small incidents. Any deployment can have unintended consequences. Fortunately, smaller releases generally result in smaller incidents that can typically be handled more readily, as they tend to be less complex and easier to isolate. In this chapter we'll discuss some strategies for further minimizing the risk of even these small incidents.

CHANGES TO THE INPUTS OF YOUR SYSTEM

Changes to the inputs of your system may also cause incidents. These can include a sudden surge in traffic, new or existing users utilizing your software in ways you didn't anticipate, and unexpected changes to or outages in third-party integrations or APIs.

Just as incidents are inevitable for you, they are for your vendors as well. Sometimes a vendor will have a severe enough incident to impact your system in a way you weren't prepared for, forcing you to declare an incident.

Your customers might also cause incidents by using your software in unpredictable ways. For example, a user may write a piece of code that inadvertently causes a flood of calls to your API, causing slowness or timeouts for other customers.

You obviously want lots of customers, but the downside of new customers using your software is that they will find unexpected ways of using your product that might cause things to break. However robust your QA and testing process might be, your customers can and will do things you don't expect, and this will result in incidents.

NONSOFTWARE ISSUES

The remainder of incidents are caused by nonsoftware issues. Creating software comes with inherent risks and pitfalls, but at least code is (ideally) orderly and readable. The rest of the world outside of our computers can be quite messy.

Happy employees can lose laptops or entry badges. Unhappy employees can publish unsavory stories that threaten your company's reputation. Global health pandemics like COVID-19 can quickly disrupt your standard business operations.

These real-world issues aren't code related, but they can cause major technical damage to your organization's ability to deliver a stable product, and thus your incident management process should account for them.

Identifying and Declaring an Incident

With any release, there are the things you know could go wrong, the things you think might go wrong, and the things that go wrong that you never even considered. That's why it's important to ensure you have the proper processes in place for identifying and declaring an incident.

There are two ways to declare an incident: automatically and manually. Both are necessary for a high-functioning incident response.

AUTOMATICALLY

For the things you know could go wrong or the things you think might go wrong, the best way to declare an incident is to have a monitoring tool identify it automatically. As we'll discuss later in the observability section, monitoring tools can be set with thresholds that automatically trigger an incident response if they are crossed. The most optimal solution would be to tie these triggers to a feature flag that can potentially disable the problematic feature automatically before the impact spreads.

MANUALLY

Observability and monitoring tools can't catch everything. In general, they are limited to catching problems that you have some ability to predict. After all, you are the one setting the thresholds and triggers that these tools use. However, there are many streams of information that can help your team identify a problem that monitoring tools would not detect. For instance, customers may tell you that a certain functionality is inoperable, either via traditional support channels or through nontraditional ones such as social media. The key is to ensure that everyone in the organization feels empowered and encouraged to reach out to relevant chat channels or support or DevOps teams and to escalate the issue as necessary.

Mitigating Risk

Let's talk about how we can minimize release risks ahead of time. The processes and tools you put in place before the inevitable incident can help to reduce the frequency and length of incidents and the damage they may cause. These processes can include:

- Managing rollbacks when needed
- Implementing kill switches or safety valves
- Planning migration strategies
- Implementing observability solutions

With the right processes in place, you can reduce the time, cost (both monetary and reputational), and damage of managing incidents. We'll explore each of these processes and offer some advice on how to establish each one effectively within your organization.

ROLLBACKS

Rolling back to a previously known working version of your software can mitigate a disruption and allow teams to troubleshoot and fix the problem. However, rollbacks can sometimes be difficult, particularly if you are releasing in large batches, or when database changes are involved. As we discussed earlier, continuous deployment can keep batch sizes small and reduce the complexity of rollbacks, but there are other solutions too. Implementing release strategies, such as blue/greens or canaries, and using feature flags can also help decrease any disruptions caused by a rollback.

Blue/green and canary deployments help minimize the need for rollbacks because they allow you to test code in production before releasing it to all users. If a rollback is needed, they also can ease the pain of reverting back to the prior version by reducing the number of impacted users. In the case of a blue/green deployment, you're not so much rolling back the change as simply diverting all traffic back to the prior working version. Depending on how your canary deployment is implemented, you may need to roll back deployed changes, but rollback is simplified by the fact that the new version and prior version coexist. Only users who've been accessing the new version will need to be redirected back to the original. While both strategies provide easier rollbacks, keep in mind that deployments involving database changes can potentially complicate either approach. If you are duplicating the database as suggested in *Chapter 1*, you'll need to ensure that any changes to the data are reconciled across the copies.

KILL SWITCHES

A physical kill switch is designed to immediately shut off machinery in the case of an emergency. The concept is basically the same when we're talking about software. If something goes wrong with your application, you want to have a way to quickly shut it down. The easiest way to implement a kill switch in software is by using feature flags.

In software, a kill switch completely disables a feature or set of features. If something isn't working, using a kill switch doesn't fix the underlying problem, but it does disable the code within the application, minimizing the damage and impact on users. This allows for a near-immediate response to an incident once it is recognized and diagnosed, without the need to perform a rollback.

The flipping of a kill switch can be triggered by humans or automation. Humans can shut off features, customers, or integrations that are causing problems whenever the need arises. This process can be automated as well, specifically when connected to application performance monitoring (APM) tools—more on that a bit later.

It's worth noting that a kill switch does not necessarily need to turn off a feature for everyone. As discussed in *Chapter 2*, feature management platforms offer extremely granular targeting capabilities that can allow you to turn off a feature for a specific subset of users affected by an incident. For example, if your application has a bug that affects only Android users, you may consider turning the problematic feature off only for Android devices.

When explaining software development and operations to less technical people, the idea that you can simply turn off something that isn't working seems pretty obvious. Feature flags make kill switches easy to implement and make the act of turning off a broken piece of software relatively quick and painless. You do not need to roll back a large part of the application by reverting to the last-known working version, which can often mean rolling back adjacent functionality. This makes the decision to disable a feature less impactful, meaning fewer approvals and fewer trade-offs, and consequently fewer delays in resolving the incident.

Turn off features for business reasons

Kill switches don't necessarily need to be limited to technical issues. They can also be used if business issues arise. Sometimes the software works perfectly, but other factors—such as unexpected demand, unpredictable weather, complexities in the supply chain, or any number of other business reasons—may necessitate shutting off access to a particular feature temporarily.

For example, a well-known fast-food chain rolled out a new item on their menu that proved immensely popular. Predicting regional demand for physical goods can be tricky, and the item sold out in some places but not others. When the item was no longer available, the company used a kill switch implemented with a targeted feature flag that turned off the menu item in the places where it was no longer available. This reduced customer frustration, as hungry customers weren't tempted by what wasn't available. Modern feature management systems have extensive user targeting capabilities that can enable turning features on and off based on configurable properties or identifiers, such as geolocation.

Kill switch case study

Kill switches don't make problems disappear, but they do minimize the blast radius and allow problems to be quietly fixed behind the scenes. To see how this works in the real world, we'd like to share an actual experience from our team at LaunchDarkly. LaunchDarkly sells feature management software that allows customers to create and use kill switches, but sometimes we also have to use them ourselves.

One time we released a feature that inadvertently caused Safari users to lose critical access for updating LaunchDarkly feature flags...on a Friday. Some organizations consider Friday releases to be a bad idea, because creating weekend incidents can lead to bad outcomes and low morale. Without kill switches, releases can have giant, weekend-destroying consequences. With kill switches, the risk of such consequences is much lower.

After the release, a customer sent us a support ticket indicating they were unable to flip feature flags in LaunchDarkly's user interface on Safari. The on-call staff confirmed the bug in our development environment and that it affected all Safari users. Once the incident was confirmed, the next step was to determine which feature was causing the issue.

We reviewed the last few things we released and found a likely culprit. Turning off the flag for that feature in our development environment restored the Safari functionality, so the team felt comfortable that turning the flag off in production would address the issue. Our support team reached back out to our customer and confirmed that the issue was resolved. Finally, we scheduled a bug fix in the next week's iteration plan to allow us to rerelease the feature.

The mood would have been quite different if reverting to the previous working version had meant rolling back days', weeks', or months' worth of changes. That would have increased the scope and impact of the incident, meaning more people would have to be involved in making the decision to roll back. This also would have taken longer, widening the impact on customers, meaning more support tickets from users who would be understandably frustrated that the issue was preventing them from accomplishing their jobs.

Remediating incidents is challenging under the best of circumstances, particularly with customers and stakeholders demanding answers instantaneously. Feature flagging helps address these challenges by offering multiple advantages over the traditional way of doing things:

- It gives you the confidence to do things that would otherwise be considered risky, such as releasing on a Friday, because it lowers the impact of failure.

- It offers much faster troubleshooting, because you can very rapidly isolate the impact of a specific change within a group of changes without redeploying in your development and production environments.

- Once the culprit has been discovered, you can leave it in a disabled state and solve the problem in the normal course of business, rather than through an emergency deployment or emergency patch. This means bug fixing becomes more routine and less urgent, and it saves on costly incidents involving numerous stakeholders.

In our case, kill-switching the release was pretty low effort and low stakes and avoided a potentially weekend-ruining situation.

SAFETY VALVES

As the name implies, a safety valve is designed to relieve pressure to avoid a potentially significant problem. Safety valves bear a lot of similarities to kill switches:

- They can be implemented in software using feature flags.
- They can be triggered manually or via automation—for instance, when connected to APM tools.
- They can disable or throttle access to a feature to address an actual or potential incident.

There are also key differences between safety valves and kill switches:

- A safety valve typically doesn't remove a feature completely but instead throttles access to it.
- Safety valves are usually associated with an external dependency.
- Because they are associated with a dependency, safety valves are typically long-lived or even permanent flags, whereas a kill switch is usually removed once a release has been deemed successful.

As an example, perhaps your application relies on a noncritical third-party service that has been having issues with performance or reliability. A safety valve can be used to help gracefully degrade the application in order to deal with the outage or availability issues. A problematic service or feature can be feature-flagged as a safety valve and triggered when certain conditions arise. Limiting access to or usage of features that rely on a problematic dependency can help avoid a larger outage.

HANDLING MIGRATIONS

Migrations involve moving from one service, software, or infrastructure to another and are notoriously risky to release. In many if not most cases, a migration is invisible to the users. This makes a progressive rollout one of the most effective ways to handle the release of a migration. A progressive rollout slowly pushes more and more traffic to the new service. While your users (hopefully) won't see the difference, it gives your team time to verify that the migration is under increasing load and revert before any potential incident occurs.

Progressive rollouts are a key use case for feature flags within a migration project. The flag can randomly assign a percentage of users to the new service. After a predetermined amount of time, if no issues arise, a larger percentage of traffic can be routed to the new service, until ultimately it is rolled out to the entire user base. While this rollout may be handled manually, some feature management platforms even allow this process to be automated.

Using feature flags and progressive rollouts for migrations can bring about larger organizational benefits as well. In many cases, teams avoid beneficial migrations simply due to the risk. Decreasing the risk of a migration can increase your team's willingness to take on such projects. This can ultimately lead to more frequent improvements to the services, software, or infrastructure that underlie your applications, which can mean they perform better and could even lower the costs of managing them.

OBSERVABILITY

Observability as applied to software systems means having the ability to ask any question of your systems to increase your understanding of a user's behavior or subjective experience without having to predict that question, behavior, or experience in advance.

Performance monitoring is not a new concept. Most organizations have well-established tooling and practices built for monitoring the status of their systems and preventing outages. Leveraging a monitoring dashboard that provides real-time insights into the general state of applications can ultimately improve your mean time to recovery (MTTR) should a problem occur.

But monitoring has its limitations. First, monitoring platforms are bound by the inputs of their users—we can only create alerts for problems we can predict. Second, monitoring is reactive. It tells us when something wrong has happened, but unless you have people proactively interpreting the data, you won't use monitoring tools to assess enhancements to your system. It's here that we can start to see the need for observability in addition to traditional monitoring.

As technology has shifted toward microservices and cloud native architectures, we've started to see the importance of understanding the patterns and interactions among components of an application. Observability is surfacing the metadata and metrics captured during these interactions and using that data to make informed decisions about changes we make to our systems. It doesn't replace monitoring; it enhances it.

By exposing observability metrics to our monitoring platforms, we can expand alerting to include specific behaviors such as request types, header values, connection protocols, and more. While your team is still required to create the thresholds, they can get increasingly granular and targeted. Additionally, adding observability to your system enables your organization to proactively assess the impact of changes, especially when combined with feature flags.

Up to this point, we've focused on feature flags as a method of incident prevention and risk mitigation. But feature flags are also a great tool for assessing the impacts of a change, especially when combined with observability metrics. Observability solutions offer the ability to capture what are called *spans* (*https://oreil.ly/ngeR3*). Spans are collections of metadata and attributes captured at each interaction between application components in a microservice environment. We can use this data to assess application performance or to identify potential problem areas.

As an example, let's say we are looking to change the connection protocol for one of our APIs. Using a feature flag, we could deploy a new version of the API that is designed to accept HTTP connections instead of TCP connections to a small subset of our users. We can observe performance metrics to see whether this change causes increased latency or results in connection errors, or just to make sure it's a reliable connection. We can also use collected span data to ensure that the right metadata is being passed to the new API or to implement a *trace* (*https://oreil.ly/35wRr*) to observe the request as it passes through various components. If the performance and metrics are to our liking, we can roll out the new change to more users.

As we discussed in *Chapter 2*, the process of incrementally rolling out a new capability is known as *progressive delivery*. Using feature flags with observability metrics is a good way to adopt a progressive delivery deployment strategy because it combines control with data. This strategy aligns with a vision for incident management wherein organizations make informed decisions about a change, measure its impact, and limit the scope of impacted users.

Principles of Healthy Incident Management

To reiterate, incidents are inevitable. Your goal should be to minimize incident severity and customer impact. In a healthy incident management process, you must adhere to the following principles:

Self-identification
> Your team aims to uncover incidents before your customers discover them.

Continuous improvement
> Incidents inform areas for continuous improvement.

Runbook operability
> Any engineer can map the problem to a runbook and execute the plans.

High volume, low impact
> Incident frequency may potentially be high, but incident severity should remain low.

SELF-IDENTIFICATION

Obviously, the ideal scenario is to discover incidents before your customers do, either automatically via tooling or manually via testing and reporting. However, this isn't just a matter of tooling; as we'll discuss, it's also a matter of forming a culture in which identifying and reporting incidents is encouraged across all teams and is not something that induces fear of potential repercussions.

CONTINUOUS IMPROVEMENT

Small incidents are a great way of uncovering which parts of your "bend, not break" system are bending the most. As your platform grows, the complexity of its codebase and infrastructure inevitably grows too. Vendors, libraries, scripts, and languages proliferate, and the ever-enlarging footprint inherently increases risk. Buttressing your system's resilience via a process of continuous improvement is crucial to maintaining stability. This requires ensuring you have a culture in which the response to incidents isn't seen as punitive and in which team members are encouraged to perform retrospectives on incidents to gather potential learnings and areas for improvement.

RUNBOOK OPERABILITY

To minimize the amount of time spent handling incidents, we recommend that you have detailed runbooks that are easily findable or even automatically sent by your alerting system. These should be easy for any on-call engineer to execute. While runbooks aren't the only solution and won't solve every problem, clear documentation that lays out the handling and escalation process can assist in spreading the burden of being on call across the organization. Expecting every engineer to master every product, language, vendor, and integration that you use is unrealistic. Clear runbooks allow all on-call engineers, rather than just a specialized few, to either resolve or escalate an issue.

HIGH VOLUME, LOW IMPACT

Low-severity incidents (loss or degradation of noncore functionality to 0%–25% of your customers) are not the primary problem. Medium- to high-severity incidents (loss of core services, data breaches, highly disruptive defects noticeable to more than 25% of customers) are the ones to avoid. While a certain degree of frequency of incidents is unavoidable, using the practices laid out in this section can hopefully help you to disable problems before they become higher-severity incidents and to learn from these lower-severity incidents so that you can prevent potential high-severity events from occurring in the future.

What Bad Incident Management Looks Like

Bad incident management is highly manual, disruptive, and stressful. Customers start noticing service outages and communicate the impact on them directly and/or publicly. Alternatively, someone on the team notices a service that might be faltering but is afraid to declare an incident. The engineer doesn't want VPs and senior leadership angrily getting involved, so the incident isn't called, and the engineer hopes the situation will resolve itself.

When the problem doesn't resolve itself, the system starts to buckle, and numerous applications begin to be affected. An incident is finally called, but now the situation is much more confusing. Lots of alerts, spikes, and warnings are flying around, and it is difficult to understand the order of failure. Your team scrambles to diagnose the situation.

Tempers start to flare. Marketing asks about the status page, account teams ask what they should tell their customers, and customer success starts asking about SLAs. Board members start getting DMs about downtime and are pinging executives. More team members are joining the #dev Slack room, trying to help but not knowing what to do first. Everyone knows that wrong decisions might be punished later, so people think carefully about suggesting solutions. Or, in the rush to quickly remediate, solutions are sometimes implemented on the fly, worsening the situation.

Scared employees become timid and wait for customers to notice the impact, the situation deteriorates, everyone is angry and confused, and the blame game is sure to follow.

What Good Incident Management Looks Like

Good incident management looks different. Your observability tools detect when a threshold is breached, and your alerting tool pages the on-call engineer. The engineer declares an incident without hesitancy or doubt, as they are unafraid of consequences should the situation later be deemed not incident worthy.

The incident lifecycle management tool opens up a new channel in your chat system and begins a timeline log for future use in a post-incident review (PIR). Armed with updated, concise, and findable runbooks, the engineer locates the relevant set of instructions and begins documenting steps taken in the new channel.

Since the engineer's organization is deploying one hundred times a day, such incidents are not uncommon. The cause is probably one of the deployments in the past hour, each being small and easily understandable. The engineer can see which ones might have led to a system malfunctioning and, assuming the malfunction was caused by a release, turns off the feature flag for that release.

Because the time from system spike to resolution was so quick, customers did not notice any downtime. Later, during the PIR and afterward, the team will look to see which applications and systems have caused the most incidents recently and will prioritize shoring up those systems.

Incidents are viewed as learning opportunities for continuous improvement. No one gets in trouble over this incident, the opportunity cost of the on-call engineer's time is minor, and the overall cost of the incident is very low.

What Makes an Incident Response Process Successful?

We've talked a lot about observability, monitoring, and feature management platforms as they relate to incident response, but incident response is about far more than just software. Let's look at the various parts of a successful incident response process.

PEOPLE

People are the single most critical aspect of any successful incident response. You can and, where appropriate, should automate parts of your incident response, but ultimately the problem will be resolved by people. That first line of defense will be your on-call staff.

There are two approaches to on-call staffing: generalist and specialist. Each approach has pros and cons, and choosing one often depends on organizational maturity. Either approach works.

The specialist approach is great, but it can be very expensive in terms of opportunity cost and morale. No one likes being on call, so having people who focus on your database, cloud computing, content delivery, and the like on call all at the same time can burn multiple people out at the same rate. The generalist approach works well also but requires clear runbooks to facilitate foolproof escalations and simple resolutions.

Your choice will likely depend in part on the size of your organization. A larger organization will have more resources for documentation and may find it easier to implement a generalist approach to help spread the burden across a large team. A smaller organization may default to the specialist approach because the expertise across the organization for resolving certain issues may be limited.

The generalist approach

A generalist approach is one that empowers anyone from the team to serve as on-call staff and to escalate incidents as necessary, regardless of their specific area of expertise. This approach lets you spread on-call duty across the team, helping to ensure that no single individual or team gets burnt out by excessive on-call duty. On the other hand, it requires investing heavily in training and documentation, as it requires that engineers be able to escalate issues outside their area of expertise.

The specialist approach

The specialist approach funnels alerts to the on-call engineer with the relevant expertise. Since domain experts receive the alerts, this approach requires a less intensive investment in documentation and training. A domain expert can utilize their expertise, often without needing to consult a runbook—and even if they do consult a runbook, the steps will make sense quickly.

Of course, it is generally not possible to have specialists always on call for everything that could possibly go wrong, so you'll need to choose areas of functionality in which uptime is most critical and/or most endangered. You will likely still need to have a generalist on call for other issues, or you can have the area experts act as generalists for the other issues.

ROLES

Ideally, incident management requires at least three roles to oversee any incident: an incident commander, a business owner, and on-call staff.

Incident commander

Incidents are confusing and stressful, which can make reaching a consensus on how to act both challenging and potentially unadvisable, as arriving at a difficult consensus can cost valuable time during an incident. Someone needs to be in charge and make decisions; that person is the incident commander.

Business owner

By *business owner*, we don't mean a founder or CEO with ultimate authority and accountability. In this case, a business owner is someone who understands the broader business impact of incident decisions, such as a product manager. The business owner is responsible for making nontechnical decisions during an incident. Examples include deciding if, when, and how to communicate the incident externally, whether lawyers need to be notified, and whether to include nontechnical employees (account managers, marketing, etc.).

On-call staff

On-call staff are the engineers who take turns being the first to handle an incident. As things can go wrong at any time of the day or night, the on-call rotation needs to work in shifts to cover every hour of every week. On-call staff should be engineers who either are specialists or are generalists who, armed with clear runbooks, can troubleshoot or escalate issues as they arise.

MANDATORY VERSUS OPTIONAL

Another decision you must make as an engineering leader is whether on-call duty is mandatory for some, mandatory for all, or optional for all. Like the specialist/generalist decision, these options all have pros and cons. Switching from one policy to another can cause friction and hurt morale, especially if the new policy is more demanding, so you should be intentional about choosing an option and stick with it until circumstances demand a change.

At LaunchDarkly, we've opted for a version of on-call duty being mandatory for some. We chose this policy because it allows for accommodation of the variety of circumstances under which on-call duty may place an undue burden on an employee, while still spreading the burden as widely as possible to avoid burnout. The ultimate decision is left to squad leaders.

As an example, at LaunchDarkly we excuse any new parents from on-call duty for the first 12 months of their baby's life. Those parents already have enough late-night pages. We give squad leaders leeway to work with people who have specific life considerations, such as primary caregiving or health concerns, that make after-hours on-call rotations particularly burdensome. Such individuals might have their on-call shifts occur only during working hours. Schedule flexibility is key to providing an inclusive workplace that allows people with differing circumstances to contribute and feel welcomed.

CULTURE

The most important thing about handling incidents is to make it cheap and easy to declare them so that even if the volume of incidents is high, they are primarily low-severity incidents. This strategy needs to be supported by a culture that recognizes the inevitability of incidents and treats them as minor events that should not inspire fear.

Any employee, regardless of their role, tenure, or status, should have the ability and confidence to surface an incident without concern for repercussions. A culture that treats incidents as normal occurrences that aren't worth getting upset about won't cause a junior employee to pause before calling an incident. This approach is an outgrowth of Toyota's application of the principles of *Kaizen*, a philosophy of continuous improvement. Heavily influenced by W. Edwards Deming, this approach focuses on the act of continuous improvement across all levels—involving everyone from top-level executives to frontline workers.

Alternatively, if your culture makes a big deal out of incidents, people will think twice about being the one to call an incident. The fear of individual attention and consequences can result in higher-severity incidents. An understanding culture might result in more false positives, but that's OK. Dealing with infrequent, extraneous false-alarm incidents is better than finding out about your high-severity incidents from your customers after the impact has grown.

In 2022, LaunchDarkly commissioned "Release Assurance: Why Innovative Software Delivery Starts with Trust and Psychological Safety" (*https://oreil.ly/ HDqiL*), a study on psychological safety and operational performance. This study found that "the majority of developers (67%) say they or someone they know has quit over pressure to minimize deployment errors, including 36% who have quit themselves." Developers are expensive to recruit and retain. Creating a culture of blame drives away engineers, costing your team money and headcount. It also creates a less pleasant working environment. And it ultimately does nothing to improve your incident response.

Accountability versus blame

A key part of establishing an understanding culture is differentiating between accountability and blame. Accountability seeks to understand the people and systems that caused something to go wrong so that similar occurrences can be prevented from happening in the future. In an accountability culture, leadership wants to find out what happened but does not default to punishing people. Software engineering is hard. If a system is set up in which a person with good intentions can make a mistake, the system needs remediation and buttressing, not the person.

Blame seeks a scapegoat to face the consequences. In a blaming culture, leadership wants to find out what happened but seeks to blame someone and have the punishment serve as a warning to others. This will lead to engineer departures and overly cautious incident calling.

Strive for an accountability culture. Happier and more relaxed employees will call more incidents more frequently, allowing for quick handling and effective learning. This cycle will continue in a virtuous loop, to the benefit of your employee retention numbers, uptime, and net promoter score (NPS).

False positives versus false negatives

In an ideal world, every incident declaration is indeed incident worthy. Sadly, we do not live in an ideal world. People will need to make judgment calls on whether something that looks awry is worth declaring an incident.

You want to err on the side of too many false positives (incident calls that turn out not to be incident worthy) rather than too many false negatives (incidents that should have been called earlier but weren't). Remember, when you are deploying continuously throughout the day, incidents are cheap. Dealing with a few marginal incidents that turn out to be nonincidents usually doesn't have many consequences. And by encouraging a culture of erring on the side of too many declarations, you decrease the chance of a real incident going undeclared for valuable minutes or hours.

False negatives are much more expensive. A delay in calling an incident means less time to remediate the incident before customers become impacted and SLAs are breached. This increases the average severity of your incidents, thus making each incident more impactful and expensive.

When handling incidents, a "fog of war" environment can cloud judgments and create stressful environments, leading to imperfect decision making. Time is a precious luxury. If you call a potential incident early, you will have more time to gather data, assess the situation, and see whether potential lightweight fixes work. If you wait to call a potential incident until it undeniably *is* an incident, you will have less time to understand and react to the situation.

Compensation

On-call duty should be compensated.

Your employees grudgingly agree to give up at least 40 of their best hours a week to work for wages. They spend time working for your organization that they could otherwise spend with loved ones or in pursuit of hobbies. Being on call threatens the remaining 128 hours in their week (or 72 waking hours, assuming 8 hours of sleep per night).

Compensating on-call duty does not adequately even out the hassle and opportunity cost of waking up in the middle of the night. Instead, it acknowledges that on-call duty eats into the hours available to live a free and relaxed life.

Compensation acknowledges the hassle of personal lives potentially being interrupted. You can pay people per quarter, per shift, or per incident handled, though consider that the latter option doesn't account for the costs to the employee even when no incident occurs. The details depend on your team and culture and will probably change over time as more employees in different time zones join the organization.

TOOLS

While people are the most critical resource in an operation, continuous delivery is impossible without relying on tools to automate tasks and amplify human efforts. Clear runbooks and dedicated tools for observability, record keeping, alerting, and incident lifecycle management help you run an efficient operation while minimizing toil.

Runbooks

While runbooks, unlike the other tools in this section, aren't a product you can buy, they are still necessary tools. Runbooks are guides that give on-call personnel step-by-step instructions on how to respond to alerts and outages. These runbooks should be exhaustive, clear, and frequently reviewed, as they need to be understood by any on-call engineer regardless of their background, with actionable steps for amelioration or escalation.

Each runbook is essentially a recipe for how to handle a particular issue. Aim for clarity, brevity, and clear and objective steps that a generalist can follow.

Runbooks should be versioned and easily findable and searchable, perhaps by keeping them in a system such as Confluence.

If your team is unsure how to create runbooks, there are many templates and guides that can assist.

Observability

As your surface area scales, the applications, integrations, and platforms that need to be monitored increase. The observability space is crowded with companies of every size to help you. Choose an API-first vendor that allows you to connect the observability tool to all of your critical systems and applications. Set thresholds that warrant attention if breached, and connect the system to your alerting tool.

Alerting

An alerting tool connects to an observability tool and sounds alarm bells if a system or application threshold has been crossed. Then the people on call are notified, and the incident-handling process commences. Similar to the observability space, there are alerting vendors at every price point for companies at all maturity levels.

Incident lifecycle management

A common industry standard for defining the incident response lifecycle comes from the Computer Security Incident Handling Guide (*https://oreil.ly/IoHF1*) developed by the National Institute of Standards and Technology (NIST). The publication sets out four phases of incident response:

Preparation
> This includes ensuring that you have the capability to respond to incidents and that you have systems and tools in place to prevent incidents from happening in the first place.

Detection and analysis
> This phase encompasses determining when an incident occurs and then assessing it to form the proper response.

Containment, eradication, and recovery
> This is the stage at which you mitigate the incident, perhaps by disabling a feature using a feature flag.

Post-incident activity
> This is a critical step in preventing future incidents, but unfortunately it's also the easiest to ignore. This phase includes things like the post-incident review.

A growing suite of incident lifecycle management vendors has emerged to help you manage this process and achieve faster resolution times and more effective postmortems. They provide visibility into when the incident started, forensic evidence documenting the situation, and a review of who was paged and when. This information is packaged into a clear timeline with action items that can assist support teams and on-call engineers in their incident response and provide a historical record for insightful post-incident reviews.

PROCESS

Incident management should be designed to remediate incidents as quickly as possible and allow for continuous improvement. Handling incidents quickly allows your team to reap the benefits of increased deployment frequency without getting bogged down in perpetual incident response mode. Some deployments will fail, and incidents will arise, but small batch sizes tend to result in small failures that, if caught early, are quickly remediated. The failures will help illuminate areas that need more attention.

Think of small incidents as being like the radioactive contrast dye used in CT scans. In general, putting radioactive materials into your body is a bad idea and should be minimized. The dye serves a useful purpose, however, as it highlights what needs ameliorating. The benefits of observability outweigh the obvious downsides of the radioactive dye.

The same philosophy applies to small incidents. They help you avoid a similar (or more severe) incident in the future by revealing which areas need buttressing, resulting in a stronger overall system.

Here's how it works in practice. An incident is triggered, sometimes by a human but ideally by your observability tool. This tool alerts the on-call engineer and connects with the incident lifecycle management tool to open a specific channel to communicate about the incident. This channel will immediately be archived after the incident is neutralized.

The initial areas of focus should be customer impact, severity level, and whether external comms are necessary. These are intricately linked. At Launch-Darkly we use the following chart to standardize incident severity and status page updates:

Severity	Update status page	Criteria	Public	Legal
Sev 0/ Critical	Yes	• Complete loss of core services. • Risk, confirmed failure, or inability to quantify scope in the availability, durability, or integrity of data affecting 25% or more of customers in the environment or instance.	Very visible event that has a deleterious effect on the brand, image, or portrayal of LaunchDarkly the company, its members or representatives, or its product, on a worldwide scale.	A set of circumstances that would constrain or threaten LaunchDarkly, its future earnings, or its ability to function.
Sev 1/ High	Yes	• Loss of core services to less than 25% of customers (but more than 10 customers) in the environment or instance. • Wide-scale, highly disruptive, or high visibility defect to 25% or more of the user base in the environment or instance. • Noticeable loss of performance in a critical area to 50% or more of customers in the environment or instance. • Risk or confirmed failure in the availability, durability, or integrity of data affecting a small number of customers.	Event that has a deleterious effect on LaunchDarkly and has a limited scale (e.g., a singular conference, statement at a public venue) such that it would reflect badly on the above and is directly relatable to LaunchDarkly. Poor press from an individual or organization that has a significant voice in the LaunchDarkly selected competitive space.	A set of circumstances that would be of significant impact to LaunchDarkly but would not jeopardize the future operations or function of the company.

Severity	Update status page	Criteria	Public	Legal
Sev 2/ Medium	Yes	• Loss of noncore services to more than 25% of customers in the environment or instance with no possible workaround. • Loss of resiliency or capacity that reduces the overall ability of the platform to manage scale. • Minor loss of performance in a critical area affecting less than 25% of customers (but more than 10 customers) in the environment or instance. • Temporary loss of the availability, durability, or integrity of data to customers.	Event that has a scope or scale that is limited to a singular small community. Poor press from a player that has moderate influence in the overall industry or space of technology.	A set of circumstances that pose some sort of issue with low impact across a wide scope *or* with high impact across a small scope.
Sev 3/ Low	Optional	• Loss of noncore functionality to less than 25% of customers in the environment or instance.	Poor feedback of limited scope from an individual or a group of individuals.	A set of circumstances that would pose an issue across a limited scope with limited impact.
Sev 4	No	• No loss of functionality. • Emergency action taken to prevent a more severe incident.		

After the on-call engineer triages the situation, they can identify the impacted service, call up the relevant runbook and follow the steps, or escalate to a specialist. Once the scope and severity of the incident have been determined, the status page can be updated using the criteria laid out in the preceding table.

POST-INCIDENT REVIEW

A post-incident review (PIR) aims to identify actions that will prevent the same class of error from happening again. A PIR should be a meta-analysis: don't just analyze the incident itself; analyze the process around the incident. Aim for an accountability culture instead of a blame culture. If a reasonable person made a reasonable decision that resulted in an incident, the system needs adjusting, not the personnel.

There will always be more ideas than are possible to implement. Identify the key pieces that are critical and focus on those. Once you've found areas to focus on, create SLAs around critical fixes. Some will need fixing now, some can go into the backlog, and some may go into the "never fix" file. In the next section, we'll discuss the metrics you can use to help you decide which is which.

If you can't identify the root cause(s) and have no confidence that the issue won't happen again, you're still in an incident state. Even if the immediate impact is resolved, the incident has not been remediated if it can easily happen again.

For high-impact incidents, you can declare a war room via synchronous chat to come up with a solution. For low- or medium-impact incidents, you can drop iteration work to focus on the undiagnosed incident and be more thoughtful about choosing teams and timing.

METRICS

Focus on the important metrics and ignore the unimportant ones. This will facilitate a virtuous cycle of continuous improvement. Focus on MTTR, response time, incident impact (number of minutes down), engineering impact (number of engineer minutes spent on incident response), dollars lost due to downtime, reputation, and staff complaints.

Do not worry about incident quantity. Ironically, incident quality is one of the most commonly measured metrics in the industry. If you have a high volume of low-severity incidents that do not harm the customer, you have a resilient system. Alternatively, if you have a low volume of high-severity incidents that result in impacted customers, breached SLAs, and lost dollars, no one will care that you had only one or two such incidents in a month.

Focus on the metrics that are much more important to track and drive down.

MTTR is the primary metric to evaluate and try to decrease. Deploying continuously throughout the day helps tremendously because of the small batch size. Since each deployment is compartmentalized, looking at the deployments from the last 30 to 60 minutes should be pretty insightful in diagnosing the incident cause. When the errant deployment is discovered, simply turn off the relevant feature flag. The time to resolution in this case would be fairly short.

Conversely, a low frequency, large-batch-size deployment cadence can be a nightmare to untangle. Which of the 40 features or bug fixes caused that particular application to go haywire? Diagnosing incidents after large deployments takes time and thus increases MTTR. Also, such deployments frequently happen in the middle of the night, so the subsequent incidents are more likely to rouse sleepy engineers or delay them from going to bed.

MTTR, shown in *Table 3-1*, is the fourth of the DORA metrics (the first three metrics were discussed in *Chapter 1*). The 2022 State of DevOps report calls it "time to restore service." The report found that low performers took between one week and one month to recover, medium performers took between one day and one week, and high performers took less than one day.

Table 3-1. DORA: Time to restore service

Software delivery performance metric[a]	Low performing	Medium	High performing
Time to restore service For the primary application or service you work on, how long does it take to restore service when a service incident or a defect that impacts users occurs?	Between one week and one month	Between one day and one week	Less than one day
[a] Adapted from the 2022 Accelerate State of DevOps report (*https://oreil.ly/iweBI*).			

The best way to improve MTTR is to institute feature flags. Once the problem is identified, flipping the flag off will instantly remove the issue from the view of users. For example, Atlassian started using feature flags and reduced MTTR by 97% (*https://oreil.ly/e2tCv*). The next best way is to have a robust observability practice, as discussed in *Chapter 4*. This will reduce the time spent trying to find the problem before flagging it off.

RESPONSE TIME

Whether you utilize a generalist or a specialist approach, you want to make sure your alerting tool is reaching the right people quickly. Time is precious in incident management, and the faster the on-call engineer is alerted, the faster they can find the right runbook and get to work.

Impact of minutes of downtime

The quantity of incidents matters far less than the quantity of customer downtime. Your customers may not know whether you had three or three hundred incidents in a month, but they will notice three minutes of impacted downtime versus three hundred minutes. The former meets an uptime guarantee of four nines; the latter meets only two nines.

Measuring the minutes of downtime gives a much truer account of the customer pain and the health of your system. Think of it as the metric for measuring incident amplitude. I live in the San Francisco Bay Area and would rather have lots of low-magnitude earthquakes than one "Big One." Your customers feel the same way.

Impact on engineering time

Engineers are expensive. They are expensive to recruit, train, pay, and retain. Thus their time is extremely valuable. Every minute an engineer spends remediating incidents is time that could otherwise be spent shipping code and increasing your organizational value. Tracking engineering minutes spent on incident management clearly defines the opportunity cost of a given incident.

As much as runbooks are internal-facing documentation, the impact on engineering time measures internal incident amplitude. Small incidents can be handled by one person quickly. Large incidents often ensnare numerous team members, and the opportunity cost grows.

Revenue lost

Lost revenue is easy to track in some organizations. B2C (business-to-consumer) ecommerce companies have a good idea of how much revenue comes in every hour. So if the checkout process is down, the cost of that incident is pretty transparent.

At B2B (business-to-business) companies, revenue per hour of downtime is harder to track. One method is to run a report in your CRM (customer relationship manager) database for opportunities lost due to an insufficient uptime guarantee. If a prospect needs four nines of availability and you can guarantee only three nines, the dollar value of that lost deal is a measurable cost. No other metric (except the next one discussed) resonates as deeply with the company's leadership as revenue lost.

Direct costs

An incident can also add costs. A typical response of a system being overtasked is to quickly add more capacity to handle the problem. As such, an incident can cause you to spin up hardware or incur hosting bills that are high and unexpected.

Reputation

Despite being somewhat difficult to quantify accurately, a good reputation pays dividends in so many ways: customers refer friends, giving you a marketing and sales tailwind; talented people want to work for you. On the other hand, a bad reputation hurts your close rate, makes recruiting harder, and is simply demoralizing. Many companies use the net promoter score (NPS) to measure reputation.

It's often easier to identify a bad reputation than a good one, since people are more likely to complain about a service they are unhappy with than to praise one they are happy with. Monitor things like negative tweets, posts, or comments on relevant sites.

Complaints about being on call

Complaints about being on call tend to track with the impact on the engineering time metric discussed previously. The former partially measures your employees' job satisfaction, while the latter measures the impact of the burden of incident response on your company.

This is another example of how continuous deployment can foster a happier environment. Employees typically won't mind dealing with many small incidents that do not have personal consequences. If you have a blame culture, on-call duty will be dreaded, and you will likely hear complaints. It's worth pointing out, though, that in a blame culture, it's not safe to assume that hearing few or no complaints means that people aren't unhappy—it could mean they don't feel safe to even surface complaints.

Noisy spikes of complaints can occur whenever on-call rotation rules shift. If you move from optional to mandatory or from specialist to generalist staffing strategies, some people will find themselves with more on-call duty than before. Be sure that you clearly communicate the reasoning behind any change in on-call expectations and how you anticipate this may impact time commitments from employees.

Final thoughts on metrics

You don't have to use all these metrics to measure the health of your incident response process; just use whichever ones fit best at your organization. Choose metrics that align with your business goals, putting the user experience first and your cost of maintaining that experience second. Ignore metrics that do not serve either purpose.

Summary

As deployments increase, incidents will also increase. That's OK. Effective incident response can weather a high volume of low-magnitude incidents. Such incidents will highlight areas of attention and allow you to continually improve your architecture before your customers are impacted.

The goal is to make incidents cheap, common, unremarkable events. You want tools and systems to declare and, when possible, remediate incidents before your customers (or even you) notice that something is awry.

In a perfect world, any incident would happen and be resolved automatically. Your observability tool would notice a crossed threshold. Thanks to an integration with a feature management platform, it would attempt to determine which of the deployments in the last hour might have caused it and then flag off the most likely culprit. It would then alert the incident lifecycle management tool to open a chat channel, notify the humans of the situation and solution, and let them see whether the situation is resolved.

This perfect-world situation is not quite a reality yet, but the vision is worth keeping in mind as you take steps to reduce the impact of your incidents. The tools, metrics, culture, people, and roles discussed will help you move closer to this state.

Have clear, versioned, frequently updated runbooks to amplify the on-call engineer's knowledge. Invest in observability, alerting, and incident management tools to declare and diagnose incidents quickly. Flag off code or vendors responsible for the incidents before your customers notice any degradation of services. Focus on metrics that center the user experience.

Underpinning (or undermining) all these incident management strategies is the strength of your culture. Foster a culture without fear for quicker response times and happier team members.

Continuous deployments, cheap incidents, and high uptime levels can all go together. Frequent deployments may lead to a higher volume of incidents but should ideally lower the overall impact of those incidents and help make them easier and faster to resolve. This will bring about learning that informs priorities to minimize future incidents. The result will be a resilient system, customer trust, employee satisfaction, and fewer interrupted bike riding lessons.

4

Measure and Experiment

Up to this point our model has consisted of deploy, release, and operate. For the final addition to our continuous operations model, we need to measure the impacts of our changes through data collection and run experiments against that data to validate whether those changes yielded the results we expected or desired. A robust measurement and experimentation practice yields treasure troves of data that can inform better product direction, reduce the risk of degradations in service, or even give an early warning sign of misaligned feature development.

In *Chapter 3*, we briefly touched on monitoring and observability solutions. We discussed that application monitoring tools often rely on reactive alerting techniques to inform operators about changes to application and platform performance. In contrast, the *measure and experiment* stage focuses on quantifying the efficacy of the features you are releasing to end users more proactively. As teams progress along their continuous operations and feature management journey, understanding the metrics that support a successful feature release—and, in some cases, support rolling back a feature—becomes increasingly important. These measurements have a direct relationship to the features you are releasing separately from your software deployment. It's necessary to shift measure and experiment practices closer to the release stage (see *Figure 4-1*).

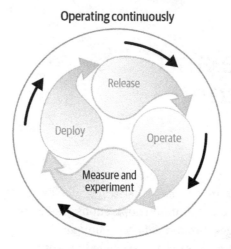

Figure 4-1. *The measure and experiment stage*

But why is measure a better solution for this stage than monitor? What should be measured, and why? What are the different types of experimentation, who should deploy them, and when should they be used? Answering these questions helps create a better understanding of how users are experiencing your service, and each answer informs what should be built next. These questions, and ultimately the practices that answer them, are especially valuable to members of the software delivery team such as product managers, who consistently find themselves asking other questions, such as:

- Does this change negatively impact a performance metric?
- Is this release "safe" to release to all users?
- Will this change help us achieve our target key performance indicators (KPIs)—e.g., cart size, sign-up rate, user click-through?

You'll note that each of these questions ties very closely to the experience of users in their utilization of the application itself. Monitoring practices are great at measuring performance-based application KPIs, such as latency or connection rate, but can't always address action-based application KPIs, such as sign-up rates or click-throughs. These action-based metrics are ones that teams want to measure, to help them understand whether revisions to their software are resulting in improvements, no change, or negative impacts.

Another advantage of measure and experiment processes is that they help remove aspects of release bias that may exist within a given feature release.

As an example, in early stages of feature development, it's easy to fall into the trap of assuming that "version 2" of your feature is a direct improvement on "version 1." However, as you reduce your batch (code push) size and increase your deployment frequency, adjustments and iterations will also occur on existing components and capabilities within your application. As a result, it's fair to assume that at a high deployment frequency, not every design decision is going to result in positive changes to the application. In other words, version 2 may not be better than version 1. Measuring and experimentation practices reduce the risk of this bias occurring by providing teams with data and quantifiable metrics that measure against predefined goals or KPIs.

Now that we've defined where measure and experiment fit into the continuous operations framework, we can start to explore the what, why, and how a bit more. In this chapter, we'll detail why measuring is a better practice for tracking/interpreting data and discuss different forms of measurement and experimentation such as feature validation, risk mitigation, and optimization.

Measure

Measure is the act of identifying, tracking, and learning from activities and events that occur within your application or from user interactions with your application. Measure includes both understanding key success metrics across release processes and experimenting with variations to understand the desired outcomes.

WHY WE NEED TO MEASURE DATA

Measuring is trying to solve for one thing: "Let's see what happened, bad or good." Either type of outcome is useful for future product decision making or risk mitigation. Measurement reflects the curiosity for validation that drives disciplines such as product management, software engineering, product design, and more. As we'll see later in this chapter, establishing a strong measurement framework and data collection strategy is a foundational component of experimentation.

Learning what worked well is a key component driving future decisions and requires that we have accurate information for our findings. Measuring something that results in greater interactions with parts of your application, or greater consumption of a newly implemented service, invites further investigation and analysis. If this new release resulted in greater engagement from users, what else can we do across the service to have a similar effect? As a contrast, monitoring might have us saying, "I'm not seeing any errors," but measuring lets us say, "Whoa, we've got a winner here, check this out."

WHAT IMPACT DOES MEASURE HAVE?

The bottom line is: understanding what increases a desirable metric or decreases an undesirable one is valuable. Perhaps adopting pagination in one part of the product increased user session length, but adding a new menu interface created confusion and increased page exits. Maybe adding pagination in other areas of the product would create additional engagement, and we should revert to our old menus. Either way, it's going to be worth it to measure further.

If we didn't adopt a measurement process and instead relied on a monitoring solution, we might miss some of these insights. Our monitoring tools' response to these changes might just be "Everything looks good, nothing broke," and then we as a product team gain no insights into how well our changes have been received.

SHIFTING FROM MEASURE TO EXPERIMENT

Up to this point we've talked about the benefits of effective measuring capabilities, but we've also talked about the downstream impacts that data can have. However, these impacts are found not only by collecting data but also by running experiments. Experiments take the data from proactively measurable events, assess how those events affect an outcome against a hypothesis, and provide insights for possible future decisions.

Experimentation comes in many different flavors, use cases, and best practices. In the next section, we will cover different types of experiments, when to use each one, which roles should be involved, why they should be utilized, and what should be gleaned. We will also discuss when monitoring, as opposed to experimentation, is the best option for specific scenarios.

Experimentation

An experiment always starts with a question and a hypothesis. The question could be something like, Which sign-up flow results in the most completions? or, What search algorithm creates the most bookings? Once a question has been established, we can form a hypothesis based on past experiences, previous data, or any number of influences. At its core, experimentation requires three essential elements: a randomized control trial, metrics, and statistics. The randomization gives you unbiased causal inference, and the statistics help you understand whether any observed difference is meaningful.

NEW SOFTWARE DELIVERY ENABLES EXPERIMENTATION

Fortunately, the evolution of software deployments has made it easier for organizations to run experiments. Back when software used to come on a CD, running experiments was difficult. Maybe you could have run an experiment by shipping different versions to different markets and soliciting feedback from users. This might have yielded some useful info for the next iteration of your software, but overall the feedback cycle was very slow.

As software delivery has evolved to become more digital and less reliant on physical copies, feedback cycles have gotten shorter, and experiments have become easier to design and run. Experiments can be run on individual features (through their implemented feature flags), deployment versions, or geographies/user groups. Results can be measured in real time, allowing for quick iteration based on the outcomes. Experimentation allows organizations to base decisions on quantifiable data from user behavior rather than on instinct, gut feelings, or prior biases.

But is experimentation really necessary? Organizations that do not have a culture of experimentation are in danger of making suboptimal decisions and missing out on learning from actual usage. They run the risk of unnecessary development cycles based on assumption-based iteration without product-informed user interaction data. Decisions are loudest voice or "HiPPO" (highest-paid person's opinion) driven rather than outcome driven. In the worst-case scenario, a release without any experimentation can result in a user dissatisfaction rollback, which is when a feature negatively impacts the user experience so much that it needs to be pulled from production. Let's walk through the structure of a feature validation experiment and where the product team fits into this type of experiment.

FEATURE VALIDATION EXPERIMENTS

Feature validation experiments let teams test features with a subset of users to determine whether that feature provides value or needs to be reconsidered. This type of experiment should happen during the release stage and can be run by product managers and/or developers.

The purpose of a feature validation experiment is to gather data from user interactions and then use that data to determine the benefits of the feature and inform future product roadmap discussions. If the new feature improves the user experience, the data will demonstrate that. If not, the insights gathered from the experiment should prove valuable for future planning. Ultimately, these experiments act as a feedback loop from user to organization and can validate whether expected user behavior aligns with actual user behavior. Understanding what users actually do when interacting with your product makes it easier to build the features that support them.

Typically it's the product managers that control feature validation experiments. Product managers are tasked with managing the production and implementation of a new feature and are measured by shipping features that impact users. Additionally, they are responsible for providing insights into why a proposed feature will have the desired impact during roadmap planning, and subsequently demonstrating that that feature had the expected impact once it was released to customers. It's a position that relies heavily on customer data and research.

In the legacy model of software deployments, product managers were forced to rely on qualitative research data from both industry and customer sources until a new feature was fully launched. It was only after the release that product managers were able to gather quantitative data on how the feature performed in the real world. Unfortunately, this came with its own set of challenges. Once a feature was broadly deployed, product managers were tasked with finding groups they could survey on their experience while also managing the fact that the entire user base was now consuming the same features.

As the software delivery model has moved forward, feature validation experiments can now be used to help product managers get new features into select users' hands faster and in a more controlled manner, providing them with data that can be used to iterate and release features with more confidence.

So how should product managers get started? The first step is to build a minimum viable product (MVP) of a new feature. The product manager should figure out the smallest, easiest denomination or divisible unit that a feature can be boiled down to and then build that specific configuration. Once it's completed, the MVP feature should be released to a small subset of users. The product manager then compares the behavior of those users with the new version or variant against the behavior of the control group. If the variant is performing better than the control against the metrics of success (more on this later), then the product manager can know with quantifiable confidence that the new feature is worth developing further.

INCENTIVE-BASED DEVELOPMENT

As is the case with any experiment, the variant doesn't always win. Sometimes the control group performs better than the new variant against a set of prescribed metrics. Many product teams may consider this a "bad" result. The consensus on the team might be, "Users didn't like that thing we built, and we wasted cycles on development!"

This is where something potentially troubling can happen. The definition of success can shift to match a more favorable outcome. What was initially viewed as unsuccessful may be reinterpreted as supporting a team's goals. This redefining of success is typically caused by a misalignment of incentives.

In some organizations, members of software delivery teams are incentivized by the quantity of shipped features, not by the magnitude of impact. Internally, shipping a big feature creates lots of fanfare among peer groups, attention from leadership, and emoji responses in the team Slack. Externally, customers notice the new feature, press releases go out touting the achievements and impact on the company, and so on. All this coverage and visibility of the release makes sense. After all, the goal of building new software is ultimately to release it to user communities, and the more features that are shipped, the greater the acclaim.

The problem with incentivizing development teams on quantity, not quality, is that there are times when an enhancement they developed has little impact on metrics that matter. Or worse, the developed item has a negative impact when compared to the current user experience. Releasing features that create a negative user experience results not only in wasted time and money (in the form of salaries) but also in lowered morale and confidence in the product's vision. No one wants to spend time working on projects that are perceived to not matter or to create adverse effects. Today, developers have a lot of choice in where they work thanks to an asymmetric labor market. Spending months working on something that lands with a thud and is quietly pulled two months later doesn't help with employee retention.

Align Incentives with Company Culture

A giant caveat is necessary here before we go any further. It's rare that teams actively and intentionally ship features just for the sake of quantity. While we are discussing the concept of incentive-based software shipping, oftentimes this happens more as a result of cultural pressure to make forward progress within an organization. I'm not implying dishonesty or nefarious actions.

Very few individuals within software communities want to work at "feature factories," where either team or individual success is measured entirely on churning out new features, regardless of their impact. While metrics or goals may be tied to release numbers, members of these teams would prefer to simply be successful in their careers and help their organizations succeed through impactful end-user experiences. Like anyone, though, developers and team leads respond to incentives that impact their careers and shift behavior to align with the stated targets. These are good people trying to make good decisions based on murky data who are beholden to certain incentives. The key to maximizing your teams' talents is to facilitate a culture in which their incentives align with those of the organization and are measured off of quantifiable data.

Teams that are tied to these types of incentive-based structures may try to "massage" the success metrics when confronted with data that shows that the control outperforms the variant. Perhaps the poor results were from a small sample size? Or maybe an unrepresentative test group? Maybe an outlier skewed the data, or the results don't align with customer interviews. In any of these cases, there could be a number of legitimate reasons that contributed to the results being worse than expected. The point here is that organizations should be careful in how they measure the success of feature shipments and should ensure that the quality of each release is being considered along with the quantity of features being released.

The presence of a healthy experimentation culture reduces the "ship or die" incentives that can color decision making. Evaluating product managers on customer impact removes the incentive to explain away bad data during MVPs.

Pitfalls of Changing Success Metrics

We all have had experiences or can likely point to examples that highlight a time when precious resources were wasted on features or products that didn't work out. One such example is from a well-known social media company.

A NEW PRODUCT IN A NEW MARKET

Facing competition from a couple of high-growth upstarts, this social media company devoted an enormous amount of resources (developer time, product managers, opportunity cost of delaying existing roadmap features, etc.) to building a new product to keep up with its new competitors. When the project reached

MVP stage, the company tested it in an international, non-English-speaking market that typically didn't draw the attention of US-based tech journalists.

To define success, the company decided to use revenue and new engagement (time spent on the feature) as the primary success metrics. If people clicked on ads and engaged with the platform through this new product, then development of the product could and should be continued.

Considerable resources were amassed and deployed, and the product was released to the test country. When the results came in, they showed that engagement on the new product was high, but revenue and engagement on the entire platform were both flat. The company was confronted with a tricky question: should it count the high product engagement as a positive enough signal that the project was worth pursuing? Or should it more heavily weigh the flat revenue and overall platform engagement metrics and refocus resources elsewhere?

Since the success metrics were new engagement and revenue, victory could plausibly be declared. Look at all this engagement on the new product! The people tasked with bringing the product to market had a powerful incentive to forge ahead. Their career prospects and internal reputation would grow if they had a major hand in developing a high-profile, impactful product.

These incentives caused them to either ignore or willfully diminish a serious problem: users were spending more time on the new product, but overall platform usage and revenue were flat. The revenue and engagement gains weren't "new"; they were cannibalized from existing products. People didn't spend more time on the company's products overall; they just shifted from the standard version to the new, novel product.

Data scientists at the company raised the alarm that the new product's engagement growth masked a lack of growth overall. If users toyed around with the new product at the expense of the rest of the platform, then building the new product wouldn't be worth the effort. Why invest so many resources to end up at the same engagement levels as the existing product?

Up to this point, everything in the story can reasonably be filed away in the "sometimes you're right, sometimes you're wrong" category. The fact that the company even tested the new product in a geographically isolated market demonstrates better-than-average operational capability.

The critical error came not in the proposal of the idea, the building of the MVP, or the limited product release. The wrong turn happened when the product team, eager to justify continued investment in the project, changed the success metrics.

FACING THE RESULTS

The product team leading this effort probably made reasonable arguments based on its own interpretations of the results. As often happens, though, personal investment in the project may have led to a biased opinion about the viability of the new product. These well-intentioned individuals wanted their project to continue, and abandoning it felt like failure. These types of influences can alter how product teams interpret the information used to make critical product decisions.

At the start of the experiment, the team defined success as meeting certain thresholds of product and platform engagement. When the results came back showing high levels of product engagement but flat levels of broader platform engagement, the team de-emphasized the platform engagement metrics in favor of the product engagement.

As a result of this revised success definition, the new product received continued investment. Developers, designers, user researchers, and product managers spent more time on the project, and it was eventually launched worldwide to great fanfare. Unfortunately, customer response was tepid. Just as the experiment data showed, the new product didn't bring in new users and instead drew most of its audience from the existing user base. Despite further investment after the troubling initial results, the product was eventually abandoned.

Overall, this was a pretty bad outcome for the company. Not only did it build something its customers didn't want and didn't use, but there was a large opportunity cost and lost resources as well. The time spent building this ill-fated product could have been better spent on other ideas or on improving other areas of the existing platform.

However, what shouldn't be lost here is that the company's idea to run an initial experimental pretest of the product was the right approach. It was the post-test product efforts and misinterpreted or misrepresented data that organizations should strive to avoid. Making incorrect guesses about user behavior is inevitable; misallocating resources after tests indicate a likely outcome is not.

An important lesson to be learned from this episode is that experimentation data is just that—data. How that data is interpreted and applied to decision making is still up to the product team, developers, and organizational leaders involved in product decisions. It's important to set success metrics that are agreed on by all the stakeholders who could be impacted by the decision to move forward with a particular project, not just by those directly involved in its implementation.

Culture and Feature Abandonment

In *Chapter 3*, we discussed how creating a culture of accountability rather than a culture of blame will improve morale, increase employee retention, and reduce incident response times. Not punishing an engineer for creating or discovering a bug makes it more likely that the next engineer will be willing to come forward with a potential bug before it becomes too problematic. Product managers and other members of the software delivery team who are responsible for shipping and releasing features should similarly be encouraged to recognize an underperforming variant and should feel safe abandoning the feature or project.

Just as you'd rather have a high frequency of false-positive incident alerts, you'd also rather have product managers move on from ideas that don't achieve early indicators of success against their control group. A common principle in the technology community is that it's better to fail fast, iterate, and improve than to lose time trying to make something perfect the first time. If individuals feel that their career, perception of their work, or even their continued employment is put at risk by abandoning an underperforming project, the likelihood of shifting the goalposts for success grows.

While encouraging this sort of trial-and-error methodology may result in fewer features being shipped more broadly when compared to an organization with more traditional shipping incentives, teams should see an increase in release impact and effectiveness. In turn, this should directly translate to a greater rate of overall success for both the employees and the product. Establishing a culture of release effectiveness and success encourages product managers and teams to gracefully kill projects to maintain higher overall product quality.

In organizations that embrace this mentality, the only unshipped features are ones that should never be shipped in the first place. Not pursuing the features that fail early tests saves time and money in the long run. No organization wants to deliver features that users don't want or won't use. The best case in such a scenario is that the new feature benefits only a small percentage of users, adding value for some users and cluttering up the menus and screens for others. The worst case is that the problematic features need to be completely removed before they frustrate a large percentage of users and slow down engineering and documentation teams that need to keep tabs on them. Shipping only those features that measure as successful enables organizations to free up developers and product teams to focus on features or aspects of a product that have the highest impact. This could mean innovating and implementing new ideas or removing stale features that lead to detrimental technical debt or product bloat.

Ultimately, encouraging product teams to trust the data in front of them creates greater agility.

Cheap Features

In *Chapter 3*, we talked about the goal of making incidents cheap and easy to declare so that they become commonplace, low-level, run-of-the-mill events that don't cause panic or problems. A high volume of cheap incidents is less costly than a low volume of expensive, high-impact incidents. With feature development, the same idea applies.

Features should have a similar cheapness to them. The likelihood that people in an organization consistently know exactly what their users want is pretty low. Utilizing data aggregation methods such as direct user interactions, surveys or interviews, or an experimentation platform that is tightly coupled with your feature management platform ensures that teams can easily run experiments to validate their ideas and helps lower the cost of features. If features themselves are viewed as cheap, then product managers will feel more comfortable abandoning the ones that underperform against control groups. It also has the added benefit of allowing these managers to prioritize organizational effort on higher-impact features.

While the idea of extending the cheapness metaphor to features is new to DevOps, the idea of not becoming too attached to things is not. "Pets versus cattle" (*https://oreil.ly/R-pRb*) is a useful analogy that has been around since the early 2010s. It describes how servers shouldn't be individually indispensable, like a beloved pet, but instead should be anonymous and easy to replace, like cows in a herd. Instead of our relying on servers that could cause enormous problems if taken offline, servers should be designed for failure and built using automated tools. If one or more servers fail, they should be unceremoniously taken offline and replaced. Having automation tools spin up and down an array of servers protects an organization from an overreliance on any one individual server.

Features will never become as identical, anonymous, and easy-come-easy-go as servers, but the "pets versus cattle" analogy still has value at the feature validation stage. Becoming less attached to a specific feature idea makes it easier for organizations to make logical, rational decisions on whether to continue or end their investment.

A/B/n Testing

We've talked a lot about experimentation, and you might be trying to fully grasp what these experiments actually look like in the wild. One of the most common experiments is A/B/n testing. As a quick refresher for those unfamiliar with it, A/B/n testing is the process of presenting end users with different variations and then assessing the efficacy of those variations based on some collected metrics. As an example, let's say that you want to see which variation of a menu bar gets the most user engagement on your website. You might create two or three different variations, randomize which one gets rendered when a user visits the page, and then collect engagement data, such as clicks, to determine which variation is best for your site. The larger the test group, the more confidence you can have about the results of your test.

DESIGNING A TEST

The first step in conducting an A/B/n test is to define the success criteria. These should be kept consistent before, during, and after the experiment. Doing so will reduce the chances that subjectivity colors the post-experiment analysis. Because of this, choosing the right criteria can be difficult and/or contentious depending on the stakeholders who will be impacted by the results. That said, most organizations typically have a small set of metrics that matter to them and could make for a good starting point; these include annual recurring revenue (ARR), monthly active users (MAUs), churn, customer acquisition cost (CAC), engagement, uptime, and cost of goods sold (COGS).

Another good practice is to keep the experiment simple. Choosing two or more metrics may sound enticing, but it also introduces complexity. Say, for instance, that you pick ARR and engagement as your metrics. An experiment on a new pricing algorithm might show an increase in ARR while also resulting in decreased engagement. Was that experiment a success? Deciding the answers to such questions after the experiment is completed lets prior narratives and incentives creep into the conversation. Being thoughtful about success criteria from the outset minimizes (but doesn't eliminate) future complexity.

The next step is to identify a test group. Test groups can be completely randomized across all users or specified based on certain user attributes, such as geographic area, user ID number, and device type. You want the sample size to be high enough that results are statistically significant and can't be dismissed due to outliers or edge cases.

RUNNING THE TEST

When it comes to running an A/B/n test, the *when* is just as important as the *who*. You want the experiment to last long enough to gather enough data to make confident decisions, but it should be short enough that it won't impede your development velocity. The experiment can be run for a set time interval or until a predetermined amount of data is collected.

As you can see, a lot goes into designing and implementing an experiment. You need an experimentation platform that offers randomization, sound statistical analysis, and tight integration with your deployment and release processes. As we mentioned earlier in this chapter, experimentation has three essential components: randomization, metrics, and statistics. You want to ensure that your platform randomizes properly based on the parameters you defined. If it doesn't, you'll be following the old adage "Garbage in, garbage out." You also want to make sure the statistics you use allow you to make good decisions. A big part of good statistics is the design of the experiment. A platform that encourages and enforces good experimental design goes a long way toward providing statistical validity.

CHOOSING THE RIGHT EXPERIMENTATION PLATFORM

How an experimentation platform interacts with your software deployment process is also important. If the experimentation platform is overly separated from your deployment process, then you introduce some risks. If the way your platform executes an experiment is too far removed from the actual deployment pipeline, the winning variant may not be implemented correctly during the actual deployment. Or if you're planning to target a certain audience, that audience targeting might not be organized the same way in the tools outside of the experimentation platform.

With well-defined success criteria, the right test groups, a clear testing interval, and a strong experimentation platform, you can run experiments and base product decisions on data rather than on overall opinions. Not to be overlooked: if your organization was previously relying on quantity-driven incentives, the cultural switch can be a challenge. This is largely due to the perception that feature shipping activity is a measure of success, but the results of this new methodology will lead to happier users and fewer surprises down the road. A/B/n testing allows you to test different versions side by side, thus letting you validate a new product idea before investing more resources in it.

Risk Mitigation

Software development is inherently full of risk. Problems can arise from any vector: your developers, your users, third-party SaaS vendors, open source libraries, and so on. Minimizing this risk is crucial to reducing incident severity and customer impact. In *Chapter 3* we talked about the importance of risk mitigation as it relates to operations, but lots of actions related to this form of risk mitigation fall outside the scope of this chapter—for example, fostering a good culture so employees don't leave unexpectedly, buying software versus building it, or adding extra redundancy into systems. For the purposes of this chapter, we're going to focus on how experimentation can be used as a tool for risk mitigation.

DEFINING RISK MITIGATION

Risk mitigation happens at all stages of the SDLC, and people in different roles take on this responsibility. The idea of risk mitigation usually brings to mind insurance: something that costs a little bit of money now in exchange for avoiding a large expenditure later. This is a useful way to think about risk mitigation. It also allows you to quantify the risk so you can decide whether the mitigation effort makes sense.

From the operational perspective, risk mitigation often comes in the form of controlled rollouts at the release stage; examples include techniques such as blue/green and canary deployments. These allow quick remediation if deployments don't perform as expected. Using these techniques, developers, product managers, DevOps engineers, and marketers all have the ability to stop a canary or revert to the blue variant when issues arise. Later in the deployment lifecycle, during the operate and monitor phases, risk mitigation comes in the form of providing site reliability engineers (SREs) with the ability to identify and turn off features or systems that are negatively impacting users.

Each of these practices (blue/green deploys, canary deploys, canary rollouts, feature flagging) can be thought of as an experiment, since each option allows for a safer fallback alternative. So how does experimentation fit in with this? Earlier we discussed how experimentation can be used to determine whether or not a feature provides a hypothetical value to users. Well, simultaneously mitigating the risk of releasing a broken feature provides value to users. So in addition to feature assessment, developers can use experimentation to determine feature viability and identify potential breaking points prior to a broader release. In other words, experimentation allows them to mitigate the risk of a failed deployment.

MEASURING RISK

The first step in mitigating risk is being able to effectively measure the level of risk for a given release. This means defining what risk means to an organization. For example, in B2B companies, risk may be quantified by calculating the value of deals that have breachable SLAs or by adding up spikes in monthly vendor costs due to incidents. At B2C companies, understanding how much revenue could be lost per unit of time inoperable gives a fairly clear quantification of risk.

These methods of quantifying risk are pretty straightforward since they can be directly correlated to impacts to the business itself. Some risk isn't as easy to quantify because it may be less tangible or have less impact on measurable metrics. That said, mitigation has a demonstrable utility for decreasing measurable risk, as well as other ancillary benefits. Increased user trust, reduced anxiety around deployments and releases, and decreased time spent on incidents may not be as easy to quantify, but they certainly have positive impacts on an organization.

Trust is difficult to measure, but it's necessary to the success of any product. Users need to trust that your service will do what it says on the box and not create unexpected downtime or degraded service. If users feel that your service creates extra headaches or additional friction, they will look for alternatives. On the flip side, users who trust your service will become champions of your platform. They might suggest new features, evangelize to others, offer feedback, or provide content that helps drive adoption up.

Like trust, reduced deployment or release anxiety is hard to quantify but provides immense value to an organization. If developers or product managers are nervous that a bad deployment or release will impact customers, create incidents, or draw angry attention from others in the organization, those employees will become hesitant to initiate deployment or release activities. Velocity will start to slow down as developers face more barriers and ship less. At some point, they may look for other jobs that allow them to ship faster.

Conversely, if you have a comparatively relaxed deploy or release cycle, positive feedback loops occur instead. Employees who aren't scared of blowback will ship faster. This will result in happier employees who recruit their network to join you, decreasing recruiting costs and bringing people in faster to meet roadmap goals more quickly. Relaxed employees can also enjoy their time off more fully, knowing that if something does go wrong, the on-call team will be able to handle it and they won't be called back to work.

We covered the benefits of decreased incident severity in *Chapter 3*. Having a culture of high-volume, low-severity incidents means fewer people pulled out of sprints, higher morale, and less distraction from priorities.

EXPERIMENTATION FOR RISK MITIGATION

So we've touched on all the reasons that measuring and mitigating risk improves an organization, but now we need to discuss the *how*. How can we use experimentation to mitigate risk? Experimentation doesn't just have to mean frontend, "pink or blue sign-up box" decisions. Experiments designed with risk mitigation in mind can reduce the risk of negative outcomes. A cloud migration, for example, is a backend use case that is not visible to most end users but can carry a great deal of risk. When undertaking something like a cloud migration, it's important to use experimentation techniques to ensure that the risks are addressed and that users will not experience negative outcomes because of something going wrong during the migration.

Migrating systems in any capacity carries a great deal of risk. That could apply to larger organizations undergoing a transition from large, on-premises legacy applications to cloud infrastructure or to smaller companies changing database systems. Risk of data loss, performance degradation, and downtime are all major concerns for these organizations. As a result, changes like these don't happen overnight; they often come as part of a large organization-wide project that consists of many moving parts. Anything that can mitigate risk during this process will be a welcome addition.

Continuing our cloud migration example, when it comes time to make the switch, the team in charge of the migration will want to build its experiment: pick success metrics, move a small subset of traffic from the on-prem system to the cloud system, and measure the results. Let's say that latency is a metric you care about. You tolerate 100 ms of latency on the on-prem system and hope that the cloud system will drop that by 20% to 80 ms. At the conclusion of the experiment, you see that latency has dropped to 90 ms—less than 100 ms, but not as big a drop as you would have liked. The purpose of running an experiment is the same as we talked about before—creating variations and testing a hypothesis—but in this case it has the added benefit of mitigating the risk associated with your migration.

Optimization

The last area of experimentation to cover is optimization. Feature validation is great for testing a small number of options against a control and/or each other, but not for dealing with more complex levels of variables. For those types of circumstances we'll need to use our experimentation framework to find the optimal outcome from that set of variables.

Optimization experiments test which option out of many has the greatest impact on a defined metric. They happen at any stage, with product managers, developers, or designers in control. We're still setting up an experiment as we have before—defining success metrics, testing variations based on a hypothesis, and measuring the result—but we're doing so in hopes of choosing the best option available, not just deciding between one or the other.

One difference with optimization experiments is in the metric definition. Success metrics in these experiments may be the same for all users, or they may differ from user to user based on personalized characteristics. For example, what is the best way to optimize a conversion flow? The answer could be very different according to the makeup of your user base.

Up to this point, we've viewed experiments as binary. A or B. New or old. The A/B/n experiments we discussed earlier work like this and have tremendous value. But these experiments work best when n represents a small number of options—say, two or three variations. With too many options, these types of tests can become unwieldy and produce data that is difficult to interpret.

When the number of variations grows beyond the point that a standard A/B/n test can handle, one solution is to leverage parameters within optimization experiments. Sometimes these experiments can be run with machine learning solutions to find the optimal outcome from a wide variety of options. Machine learning algorithms such as a contextual multiarmed bandit, which allows multiple variations to be tested and sends more traffic to the successful variation as time goes on, will try different combinations of the provider variable set to learn which combinations work best in different circumstances.

Setting broader parameters allows machines or humans (developers or others) to change the way an experiment is being run without altering code. Product managers, marketers, operations teams, and others can test small changes in the variations that affect the users without needing developers to push new code configurations. This frees up developers to focus on their next sprint and lets the people who are closest to the users and know them best make the decisions.

Experimentation Examples

We've talked a lot about experimentation in the abstract sense, but what does this actually look like in the real world? Let's walk through a handful of examples that illustrate the power of adopting the experimentation framework that we laid out in this chapter.

MEASURING A SIGN-UP FLOW

For our first example, let's look at a typical sign-up flow. A sign-up flow has two goals: to have the highest possible number of users complete the flow, and to extract the most information from the users. Unfortunately, these two goals can sometimes conflict with each other. Having fewer questions decreases the friction in signing up and results in more sign-ups, but adding questions to the sign-up flow means gaining a greater understanding of each user. Both are important goals, but they can negatively impact each other and require a certain balance.

A lot of variables can impact these goals: the number of questions, the placement of the sign-up box, the color of the sign-up box, the color of the sign-up font, the inclusion of an exclamation point (*Sign up!*), the number of questions asked of the user, the order of the questions, which questions are mandatory, and so forth.

With this many variables, and with so many unknowns about who visits the sign-up page, how can anyone reliably know which questions to include and which ones to make mandatory? Will the answers change based on the user's geography, referral source, or history on the site? With many variables come many possible answers—too many for A/B/n tests to measure.

Enter optimization experiments. Creating an optimization experiment that leverages a machine learning solution, open source tools like Ax, and hosted SaaS services as examples lets organizations utilize machine models, which will become increasingly robust as the technology develops. Organizations can set parameters that let machine learning models try out all the options to see what works best. In this example, you can have parameters for all these options and let the machine learning model try them in all the different combinations. The model will discard combinations that don't perform well and try ones that do perform well against one another. This process will be repeated at scale until at the end you have an optimized set of results.

The parameters need to be set up by engineers who understand how to manipulate the experimentation platform. Once the setup is complete, the reins can be handed over to others to run. In the sign-up flow example, product managers or marketers might be best suited to run the optimization experiment.

FIFTY SHADES OF BLUE

Another relevant example of experimentation from Google is its "50 shades of blue" experiment (*https://oreil.ly/P58mo*). When Google launched Gmail, it had blue ads on the right sidebar. But there are many shades of blue, something you've likely encountered if you've ever gone to the paint section of a home improvement store. Which blue would entice more users to click? Anyone could have guessed, but no one knew.

So Google tested 40+ shades of blue, trying out each variation with 1% of its users. The data showed that a shade of blue with a slightly purple tint outperformed the other options. The implementation of this specific blue into the ads resulted in $200 million in additional ad revenue.

Not every experiment will lead to $200 million in measurable impact, since not every product operates at the scale of Gmail. Still, every team has goals to hit and metrics to surpass, and optimization experiments can surface better options than would opinions, hunches, or guesswork. Improving the sign-up form conversion rate by 2% has a measurable impact as well. Continually stacking 2% improvements on top of one another adds up.

Machine learning was not used widely outside of academia when Gmail launched, so the world of testable combinations has greatly expanded since Google ran its experiment. If the experiment were to take place today, the color of the ads could be combined with the font, size, and character length to further optimize for the highest click-through rate.

Summary

Let's recap what we've covered in this chapter. Good measurement practices are the first step toward understanding and the foundation for experimentation. Creating a culture of experimentation for product validation, risk mitigation, and optimization allows organizations to make decisions based on data rather than on opinions. Last, modern experimentation platforms allow cohesive, heterogeneous teams to test hypotheses and make better decisions across the entire operational process.

We've illustrated where measuring and monitoring start to diverge in purpose. Whereas teams used to rely on SREs to monitor systems in case something bad happened, now developers and product teams can run experiments that inform their next steps before something goes wrong. While experiments should happen concurrently at all stages of the SDLC, monitoring was confined to the final stage in the ops process. The measure and experiment stage is a critical step for modern software delivery pipelines.

Measurement and experimentation enable teams across an organization to take proactive steps to test new capabilities and allow them to create a framework for how new features and products can simultaneously be rolled out while also mitigating risk. The takeaway here should be this: create a strong system for measurement to track and collect data, use those measurements to determine success metrics, create a hypothesis based on those success metrics, and run experiments to prove or disprove the hypothesis.

Conclusion

We hope that in reading this book you have learned best practices, pitfalls to avoid, and ideas you can use for operating continuously. *Effective Feature Management*, the book that predates this one, was published in 2019—a lifetime ago when compared to today (2023). Still, *Effective Feature Management* remains an excellent primer and foundation that enables operating continuously as described in this book.

This book opened by discussing the ways in which the software delivery process represented in the DevOps infinity loop needs updating when compared to the way organizations and teams must operate today. Advancements in processes, cultures, and tooling have driven an evolution across the software delivery landscape. The idea of an "integrated software development team" has become more widespread, and there is tighter collaboration now among teams that were traditionally siloed. Teams such as design, product management, security, engineering, and operations now work more closely with development teams not only to build and ship software but also to ship better experiences and outcomes for their audiences.

The interactions of these teams and their responsibilities are no longer represented by sequential handoffs and instead are run as continuous processes across the entire landscape. This is *operating continuously* (see *Figure C-1*).

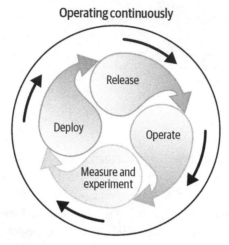

Figure C-1. Operating continuously

Rethinking the Loop

The right side of the infinity loop model, composed of release, deploy, operate, and monitor, no longer accurately reflects the model that organizations should be working to achieve. Definitions in these individual stages have changed, and in many cases these stages are executing in parallel to the latter stages. The right side of the loop fundamentally shifts to reflect activities and processes that keep systems healthy and can respond quickly and deliver change.

With the growth in cloud and SaaS platforms, software has moved away from the rigid annual-release process and is now predominantly built on demand as code is shipped. The deploy phase leads off the new model because operating these new software platforms ultimately begins by delivering the code to where it will run. A process that formerly took place once every few months can now take place multiple times an hour in mature organizations.

DEPLOY

As discussed in *Chapter 1*, this model of having smaller and more frequent releases has several benefits:

- Small batch sizes
- Easy problem diagnosis
- Speed to market

- Merge conflict minimization
- High team morale

On the other hand, the inverse of these points can be true for large and infrequent deployments, which often result in increased complexity and risk and ultimately can impact the job satisfaction of the developers involved.

The act of deploying software (taking the compiled code and shipping it to infrastructure) needs to be separated from the process at which we release that software to end users and systems (which is why the new model places the release stage directly adjacent to deployment). This separation allows us to take the "smaller and more frequent releases" methodology and apply it to the way users consume features within a software platform. In the previous model, once a deployment was completed (i.e., the software was loaded onto its destination), the software would be released in its entirety to consumers. Strategies such as blue/green deployments and canaries have tried to mitigate the risk of this process, but approaching these strategies through an infrastructure lens is highly complex and problematic.

RELEASE

By separating release from deployment, teams can leverage tooling such as feature flags and targeting rules to apply these rollout strategies at a feature level. The act of continuously configuring these release strategies, leveraging kill switches to disable or roll back problematic code, and gradually expanding the size of a deployment represents how the release process is now the most effective way to ship features to end users, becoming a continuous motion in its own right.

In this model, organizations are continually making adjustments across their application releases to ensure the right teams are getting the right features at the right time. These same principles apply to the operations space, as the continuous release and deployment stages can directly influence the creation and management of incidents.

OPERATE

Consider that in the traditional model, a great amount of care and effort goes into ensuring that all the ranges of testing and validation are completed before the software is deployed out. If you are increasing your deployment velocity, it's only natural to assume that there is an increased risk profile for incidents coming from those changes. In our updated model, where we embrace a continuously operating posture, this risk, as discussed in Chapters *1*, *2*, and *3*, is effectively mitigated by (1) making the changes much smaller and (2) controlling the way that these features are released to end users through the use of tools such as feature flags and advanced release strategies such as canary deployments. With controls like these in place, mitigation of an outage incident is as easy as disabling the feature for the impacted user community, as opposed to rolling back the entire deployment.

MEASURE AND EXPERIMENT

The ultimate success of any software is whether and how it's used. Incidents and outages are an initial but insufficient way of determining the overall success of a software delivery organization and the features it is shipping. Mature organizations approach the release of software through the lens of data. Leveraging existing measurement frameworks such as DORA, coupled with a culture that measures and proactively experiments with the features being released, ensures that the right goals are being reached while also managing risk. This process isn't a onetime activity. In reality, as software is continually deployed, released, and operated, these practices are continuously measured and experimented against throughout the entire lifecycle.

Is the new login process successfully guiding your user community in the way you wanted it to? Has the new feature resulted in users engaging with your product in the ways you hypothesized it would? Teams often fall into the habit of considering the development and deployment of a feature as "success." However, organizations should leverage data to guard themselves against continuing to ship features that aren't achieving their goals, KPIs, and overall strategy.

The results of the measure and experiment stage should directly influence how teams are releasing. Successful experiments should result in an acceleration of your release process, growing the cohort of users who are consuming your new capabilities. This is a great example of how the operating continuously model influences each stage—often in nonlinear ways.

Final Words

Software processes, like software itself, are constantly evolving. The model of the DevOps infinity loop and its approach to the modern software delivery lifecycle have given organizations a path to adopting processes that accelerate how value is delivered to organizations. It's only natural that as teams adopt these processes, their skill and experience increase, and how teams operate together improves and expands. This increased skill results in an increased velocity and, in many ways, increased demand from the business. Couple this with the shifts in the ways we work, the adaptability of the cloud, and the increased quality of tooling and solutions, and organizations arrive at a place where they've evolved beyond what the existing model can allow.

This book has explored this evolution from the perspective that teams are evolving into a model where the stages of the infinity loop have changed—with some being replaced entirely by new stages. This new model reflects how organizations are moving beyond the traditional process-driven, sequential model and into the operating continuously model, where all these tasks are happening everywhere across the organization, all at once.

Happy shipping!

Index

About the Authors

Edith Harbaugh is the founding CEO of LaunchDarkly, the leading feature management platform. She's an international speaker on effective feature management patterns and software development. She's worked in engineering, product, and marketing at small and big consumer and enterprise companies, most recently at TripIt and Concur. She holds multiple patents from her time at Epicentric.

Cody De Arkland leads the developer relations team at LaunchDarkly and has been working in operations, engineering, and marketing roles in the technology space for over 15 years. His passions include development frameworks, enterprise automation, content creation, and reducing builder friction.

Brian Rinaldi is a developer experience engineer at LaunchDarkly with over 20 years of experience as a developer for the web. Brian is actively involved in the community running developer meetups via CFE.dev and Orlando Devs. He's the editor of the *Jamstacked* newsletter and coauthor of *The Jamstack Book* from Manning.

Colophon

The cover image is by Susan Thompson. The cover fonts are Guardian Sans and Gilroy. The text font is Scala Pro and the heading font is Benton Sans.

CPSIA information can be obtained
at www.ICGtesting.com
Printed in the USA
JSHW011746210423
40690JS00003B/6